FROM START-UP
TO CLEAN-UP

It continues to be a source of delight to know that "how to" material for laity is and continues to be made available, that excellence, thoroughness, and results might be attained for the Kingdom of God. Carol's work is educational, practical, and thorough. A must for those involved in the special event plans for their church or organization.

Pat Clary
Executive Director
The National Women's Ministries Institute

FROM START-UP TO CLEAN-UP

CAROL OCKERT TREACHLER

VICTOR BOOKS®

A DIVISION OF SCRIPTURE PRESS PUBLICATIONS INC.
USA CANADA ENGLAND

Scripture quotations are taken from the *King James Version*.

Library of Congress Cataloging-in-Publication Data

Treachler, Carol O.
  From start-up to clean-up / Carol O. Treachler.
    p.   cm.
  ISBN 0-89693-199-4
  1. Church entertainments. 2. Church dinners.   I. Title.
BV1620.T74 1991   90-19255
259'.8 — dc20   CIP

1   2   3   4   5   6   7   8   9   10   Printing/Year   95   94   93   92   91

CONTENTS

Dedicated to

The Lord,
the ultimate creative thinker.

To my family,
who listens to my thoughts . . . endlessly.

To Dan Penn,
my pastor in Texas,
who held me on a loose leash.

To Lori, Faith,
and
the ladies of Garland Bible Fellowship
who gave me opportunity
and encouragement in discovering
how to put on successful special events.

SECTION ONE:
Strategy

ONE

The Purpose
of Special Events

The candlelight flickers. The air is washed in soft music. Lacy paper snowflakes sparkle silently overhead. You are tired but you are so glad you came. The fun is pure, clean, and crazy. You laugh until your sides ache at the skit put on by that zany George. You get a chance to chat over dessert with the new couple you've been wanting to meet. And you catch your spouse looking at you with dreamy eyes in the candle light. You feel refreshed, encouraged, and a bit challenged. You are at a special event and it is working its magic on you.

Special events are very important in the life of a church. Through this wonderfully creative medium things can be accomplished that would be impossible to do as effectively in a normal Sunday morning service. A shower can launch a bride into an exciting new life. A couples' retreat can give a husband and wife with a troubled marriage the time and atmosphere to start afresh. A ladies' luncheon can introduce the Lord to a God-starved soul. So resist the temptation to think of special events as frivolous or quasi-spiritual. God can accomplish many great and mighty things through special events.

The Goals of Your Special Event
Sense of unity. Special events are valuable in the life of a church for the same reason that birthday parties and Christmas traditions are important to a family. They give the local congregation a feeling of identity and a sense of belonging. This in turn

fosters a group commitment. People start to think of themselves as part of the church rather than simply viewing the church as someplace they attend once a week. The church stops being "them" and starts being "us."

Instruction. Special events can be used very effectively to teach spiritual truths. People learn by what they see, hear, taste, touch, and smell. A banquet provides a situation where all five senses can be used to communicate a spiritual lesson. The Lord used this method of instruction in the Old Testament when He set up the feast days. The Passover is a prime example of the Lord using the ear, eye, and mouth gates to impress upon the Children of Israel a remembrance of what He had done for them as well as imprint the picture of redemption.

Celebration. Special events can provide times of rejoicing. Holidays, weddings, and even mortgage burnings need a setting where people can lift grateful and happy hearts to the Lord.

Honoring. Special events can honor those who have reached milestones in their lives. These events, which can take the form of anniversary parties, showers, graduation banquets, Mother's Day programs, and the like, accomplish the goal of making people feel loved and supported. It is an encouragement to share these special times in life with our church family. Because God has designed us to be interdependent, sharing the joys of life tends to multiply the happiness.

Evangelism. Special events can provide an excellent opportunity to share the Gospel with those who do not know the Lord personally. Inviting a friend to a luncheon is nonthreatening and allows the visitor to meet Christians in a relaxed atmosphere. Many times special events will stir up questions in a friend's mind that will have life-changing impact. People who would never darken the door of a church on Sunday morning might consider going to their grandchild's Christmas program or a neighbor's spring luncheon.

Recreation. In Deuteronomy 14:22-26 the Lord in His infinite wisdom commanded His people to take a portion of the money given to Him and use it to have a party. The Lord who created us knows that we need wholesome, fun times of recreation. As with everything that is pleasurable it must be kept in balance so that the work of the Lord is not hindered. But times of recreation are refreshing and positive, so providing this function for the children of God is a worthy and proper goal. If not at church — then where?

Worship. Special events can also provide a time to get away and worship the Lord. Early morning at a camp retreat, a heart-to-heart sharing and praise time at a ladies' luncheon, a sweet singing time at a Sunday School social: these are all examples of moments in time where true worship of the Almighty can happen.

Fellowship. Special events help people get acquainted. This is especially true if the event is structured to encourage interaction. People are usually not given the time or opportunity on Sunday morning to meet and hold long conversations with each other. It is hard to walk up to strangers and engage them in discussion. A special event, especially the kind that offers several mixers, creates an atmosphere conducive to becoming better acquainted.

Work projects. Special events can be used to gather a group of people for the purpose of accomplishing a project. Painting a building, raking leaves, or decorating for Christmas can become much easier if there are many folks helping. Sometimes adding a contest to a work day can change the *job* into a *challenge.* People can be so busy having fun that they might not even realize that they are working!

Stimulating interest. Special events can also be used to focus attention on a specific need or concern. Do we want to urge our people to pray for missions? Are we trying to get them excited about what is going on in the youth ministry? Are we hoping to instigate a desire for the women to attend a ladies' Bible study? A special event can stand up and shout, "Look here! Look here! Something is happening that you will want to know about!" This is especially critical when starting a new phase of a ministry. Kick-off events are great because they say, "It's here! It's now! Get involved!"

Fund-raising. Sometimes a special event can be used to raise money for a particular project. The function can concentrate attention on a specific need. Be careful not to overdo the fund-raising goal lest the testimony of your church appear commercial.

Relationship building. Another often overlooked purpose of special events is that they can be used to build relationships.

11

When people work with each other on a project, they get to know each other. The event gives them something in common. They usually meet outside of formal services and discover other areas of similar interest. While people can become acquaintances on Sunday mornings, they can become friends working on special events.

Gift development. God has given a myriad of gifts and talents to His people. He tells us to use them for His honor and glory. He is overjoyed when these talents are developed and given back to Him as an expression of worship. This not only honors God but it gives purpose and meaning to the craft or talent. There is a man at our church who has spent most of his time at the last several church picnics giving people boat rides. He takes great satisfaction in sharing his boat, yet he is serving God by helping us!

A Chance for People to Grow

Special events can also allow people to try different tasks to see where their talents lie. If people are never given a chance to sing, how will they know that the Lord has given them a voice? By not using a hidden talent they are missing out on blessings. Having a successful experience can open new vistas. I remember the first time I was asked to do the decorations for a banquet; I was fifteen and petrified. But as I was making snowman centerpieces out of caramel popcorn balls, I realized how much fun it was to see my wild ideas become reality. God wants His children to stretch out and utilize all the potential He has tucked inside of them.

We may sometimes think that the only way to serve God is by teaching or singing, these being the "traditional" up-front gifts. This, of course, is an incorrect and limiting mind-set. After all Dorcas, of New Testament fame, served God by sewing. We can serve God by cooking, painting, arranging flowers, or whatever. All talents are valuable. There is much joy in serving God with the gifts He has bestowed on us. Let the feet rejoice in being feet; let the hands rejoice in being hands. It is the meshing of the talents of the body of believers that makes an event spectacular.

TWO

Pitfalls
in Planning

As in all endeavors worth doing, the road to successful events is strewn with various errors, mistakes, and pitfalls. Recognizing these common blunders is the first step in avoiding them.

Mixed up priorities. In the heat of preparations, when the pressure is on, it is very easy to get priorities mixed up, and as a result, feelings get sacrificed on the altar of success. How can the Lord be pleased when people have been needlessly hurt? It is much like a child presenting his mother a bouquet after blackening his brother's eye to obtain them. So a balance must be maintained between having a dynamite event and never forgetting that *people are more important than the event.*

Communication. The biggest difficulty in most special events is the problem of communication. This happens when the person in charge does not do an adequate job in letting the helpers know what is going on. The committee heads need to have a general idea of the big picture so that they can tailor their plans accordingly. Everyone should also know who is in charge of what. It is important for everyone involved to know who to contact to get a meaningful answer. This should short-circuit a lot of runarounds and keep the avenues of communication clear. The publicity people need to know who is in charge of the agenda so they know who to get in touch with to find out what attractions they should put on their posters. The decoration committee might need to discuss with the food committee where would be the most convenient spot for the buffet table.

A result of poor communication is a problem called *expectation variance*. This takes place when people don't understand what is expected of them. When this happens people either make conflicting plans or a job gets left undone. Both the food committee and the decoration committee might think it their job to buy the cups, or worse, each might think the other is taking care of it and thus no one would get the cups. To avoid tension, hurt feelings, and resentment, people must understand very clearly the scope of their responsibility.

Chaos. Chaos is a lack of organization. I have heard people say, "Let's keep it simple" and try to run an event without any organization. It ends up being more of a headache because when proper plans are not made, people do not know what their jobs are or who to talk to for answers. People end up dashing around like mad at the last minute. Important things are forgotten. The event looks thrown together. If an event is worth doing, it is worth doing well. "Whatsoever ye do, do it heartily, as to the Lord" (Col. 3:23). This does not mean everything has to be a big production, expensive, or even complicated, but it must be thought out and some simple structure developed so that the event can function smoothly.

Personality clash. Christian maturity is a process. Because the world and the Christian community are made up of imperfect human beings, problems inevitably arise. One such problem occurs when personalities clash. A coordinator should be on the lookout for this problem and seek to help. How? Of course, prayer is an important first step. Sometimes gentle confrontation is necessary. This is why it is wise to get the committee heads to recruit the people they feel comfortable with, while at the same time encouraging them to include one or two people who are not too involved. Place a person with a known personality problem with a spiritually mature individual who will use both love and firmness.

The Problem of Burnout

Burnout happens when a person has been involved in an event that has not been properly planned. They needed help and were not rescued. They got left holding the bag and remember the whole experience with a shudder. On occasion it can happen when a person has been taken advantage of or overworked.

14

Burned out people lose their vision because they are too tired to perform. Sometimes tension, ingratitude, or lack of encouragement can push the process of burnout along. Only by the grace of God will these people agree to take on an endeavor again. It is much easier to prevent burnout than to fix it. So make sure you rescue people when they look tired, stressed out, overwhelmed, or when their sense of humor is fading, or their joy is not evident.

You rescue people by either providing more help or lightening the work load, either taking the job on yourself or deleting the task altogether. All this must be done without recrimination; usually people who are overwhelmed feel guilty enough. Try to make sure that all involved have a reasonable load and that they succeed at what they attempt.

People do not like feeling incompetent and will not sign up for another chance to fail. When trying to get burned out people back in the saddle again, start off very slowly with small, well-defined jobs. Make sure they have a good experience if they say yes, but expect that they will give you some hard-to-take noes. Usually after several small successful experiences people are more willing to volunteer and help.

So, how about you? How do you protect yourself from burnout? None of us is immune. I tend to overload myself not because I have to, but because I get so excited by each new project. Then I start feeling overwhelmed. I lose sleep, find myself shaking, and catch myself snapping at my children. So I either have to backtrack and get out of a commitment or gut it out. This is not the ideal way to handle the burnout problem.

Everyone says that you have to learn to say no. I quite agree, but I find that the person I really have to say no to is *me!* When *you* feel the telltale overcommitment signs start to pop up in yourself, resist the urge to say yes to anything else. I don't care how intriguing it sounds! Back off as best you can, delegate another piece, or beg off that event that you gave a tentative yes to. Give yourself some space to maneuver.

When coordinating an event try to work yourself out of a job by delegating all major tasks. This is usually not a problem for people who are natural administrators; they do this already. But delegating is very tough for a creative idea person. Any coordinator needs to be free to rescue other people and to put out the fires that will inevitably start. Learn this or die. You cannot help others when you are drowning yourself.

More Pitfalls to Avoid

Procrastination. At all costs do as much as possible, as soon as possible. This gives you time to work out the snags. When things are put off to the very end, people feel rushed and pressured. This gives them a bad experience and may contribute to burnout. Avoiding procrastination can greatly reduce everyone's anxiety level.

If last minute work crops up, the procrastinator has no time to deal with it. Once I did a banquet where I was expecting fifty to seventy-five people. The last week of registration we had a flood of people sign up, more than doubling the projected attendance. I was very glad that I had done most of the work early because I had to scramble that week rearranging my plans to accommodate the extra numbers.

Procrastination also shortchanges the event because people do not have the time to put in the extras. Start early enough to give people flexibility and the time to come up with creative ideas. This is especially true if you have a large group of people working on a project. It takes more time to move a host of people than to move a few.

Technical accuracy. Make sure that all written words involved with the event — on posters, programs, or signs — are scrutinized for errors. Spelling, grammatical, and typographical errors make an event look shoddy, and the tremendous time and effort of many individuals is marred.

Take nothing for granted. It is worth the trouble to check and make sure things are where they are supposed to be. This practice will help you avoid the horrifying experience of being caught unprepared. Many items, such as paper plates and cups, are standard stock in church kitchens, but it is still best to make sure that the kitchen does not run low the day of the event. Otherwise one hundred and fifty hungry guests may have to sing Christmas carols while someone dashes to the store to buy paper plates. (Lest you think I jest, yes, this happened to me!)

"I'd rather do it myself." It is a real temptation, especially if you are gifted with an ample supply of creativity, to try to do the

whole event yourself. I fight this in myself all the time. It is almost physically painful for me to give up large chunks of responsibility to others. After all, if you do it yourself, you know it is getting done. You then have total creative control, not to mention that enlisting help can be a long and painful process. Conquer the urge to do it all by yourself, however.

The more people involved, the more resources from which the event has to draw. One person may have a flair for decorations, another for coming up with skit ideas, and another may be a great cook. Tapping into many peoples' time and talents allows for results that are impossible for one person to achieve alone.

The more the work is dispersed the less work any one person has to do. Spreading out the work load is the best protection I know against burnout.

Even more important, when people work on an event, they put something of themselves into it. This tends to increase their commitment level. It is no longer something the church is putting on. It is "theirs." They will be more willing to come and more willing to invite their friends.

Special events can and should be used to involve people who are new to the church, not well-known, or not very active. Giving them an opportunity to work on an event can help them make new friends and give them a sense of belonging to the group. Sometimes people are not involved simply because they have not been asked.

How to Get the Help You Need
So how do you go about drafting help? This is by far the most difficult, threatening part of doing any special event. The key to enlisting help is to enthusiastically enable other people to catch the vision of the event. They need to see the potential of what God can do in a particular area. Once people get interested they will want to be on the team.

One ounce of enthusiasm is worth a pound of guilt. It is so easy to put pressure on people to do what they "ought" to be doing (which is serving God by helping me)! You, however, are not the Holy Spirit; let Him work to change priorities, not you. Search for the helpers that God has given to you. Do not motivate by guilt. Instead, seek to motivate people to assist you out of love for the Lord. If people feel manipulated and forced to do something that they really do not want to do, tension and resentment build. The resulting atmosphere is detrimental to the function, dampens the joy, and poisons the mood.

Your attitude is crucial in achieving a successful event. It is important not to look at doing an event as a chore. The people working on the event will mirror the attitude of the leadership. They will be robbed of great joy if they adopt a "Why do I get stuck with all the work" attitude. To be able to serve the Lord is more than a duty, it is a privilege. The most high God wants to use us. How fantastic! Those who help reap temporal and eternal rewards. Why force people to eat ice cream? Remember Tom Sawyer and his fence? The trick is to encourage people to *want* to be involved.

Nothing replaces personally asking people to help. Many times people will be willing to sacrifice if they feel wanted and needed. People will not be willing to help if they think that their help is inconsequential. But be sure to give them a face-saving way to decline. For example: "We could use your help with decorations. We hear that you have a gift in this area. Do you have the time to help us, or is your schedule too tight?"

Sometimes you will receive negative responses, some given in a devastating manner. Expect it. Sometimes it takes me several days to recover from an unkind no. This is the biggest single fear that keeps people from enlisting others. How do we deal with this problem so that it doesn't hinder us from accomplishing what God has for us to do? I try to shield myself from the pain of rejection by prefacing my request with the phrase "but you can say no." Somehow, my giving them permission to say no helps to protect me from feeling presumptuous. So I'll say, "Have I got a job for you! This is really neat and you would be perfect for it. But you can say no; I'll understand." Many times when people have to say no they feel bad that they have to reject you, so they will go out of their way to tell you how busy they are. Or they tell you angrily that people are expecting too much of them. This has the effect of making you feel like a rat to have asked. When this happens maintain your gracious mien, work on forgiving them, and resist the urge to judge their spiritual maturity or commitment level. Keep in mind that you do not know the whole picture—you do not know what difficulties these people are coping with at this particular time.

Just remember when *you* have to say no, do it compassionately. The best noes that I have ever received sound something like this: "I'd really love to, it sounds so exciting, but you have caught me at a bad time. Ask me again at another time." I could kiss these peoples' feet.

Ideally the coordinator should line up the committee chairpeople as soon as possible. The committee heads then enlist people to help them. This way they can gather a group of people they can work comfortably with and in whom they have a degree of confidence. The idea is to have many people drafting, not just the coordinator. The more people drafting the more involvement. This works because people are more willing to help a friend than an acquaintance.

The coordinator should make sure that people new or not involved are personally asked to help. Put them into committees where they can get to know others. This will stretch out any cliques by introducing new blood. Establish in the minds of your leaders a ministry mentality. They should be encouraged to build relationships in their small group as well as accomplish the departmental goals. This is "hands on" discipleship!

If trouble is found filling a leadership position on a committee, it sometimes works to go backward. First find people to take the smaller tasks and then find someone to supervise it once all the recruiting is done. Some folks do not mind overseeing a project but are reluctant to tackle the drafting aspect. This can work effectively but should be used only when leadership cannot readily be found.

Sometimes help can be obtained with a general call in the church bulletin or by an announcement. Though this method may not get much response, it is an important step because it lets the congregation know that the event is not being put together by the "chosen few." Do not, however, advertise select leadership positions. For example, don't use the bulletin to ask for someone to direct the Vacation Bible School; ask for anyone who wants to work with the Vacation Bible School ministry. This gives you some flexibility to place people where their gifts will best be used without having to reject them. Remember this is a church, with volunteer labor, not a company that interviews applicants. The volunteers should not have to risk rejection simply because the leader is afraid of being refused.

Another tip for enlisting help is to use established groups. Ask the junior high kids to wait on tables or the senior high group to organize the baby-sitting. Ask the ladies' Bible study group to sing or the missionary group to give a presentation. Usually, these people are more willing to say yes because they work as a group and the weight of responsibility does not lie on any one individual's shoulders.

It is important to keep track of people's talents and hobbies. Find out and remember those who excel at art, cake decorating, and flower arranging. Generally, people are delighted to use their particular gifts for the Lord.

On occasion someone may feel that he or she is being taken advantage of. This is especially true if someone is famous or earns his livelihood with whatever craft or talent you are seeking. You may want to consider compensating this person monetarily. If so, say so the first time you approach him or her. The person may well turn the offer of money down but you have not been presumptuous in the process. Sometimes just batting the question around will work: "I am looking for about two dozen daisies for our upcoming luncheon. I understand that you are a florist. How much would it cost us to get them from you?" This kind of question gives people the opportunity to set a price they consider fair or perhaps offer their services free of charge. In any case you have not presumed upon them.

One way to discover talent is to send around a talent sheet. Do not ask people if they *can* decorate a cake or if they are *good* at painting. Ask them if they *enjoy* doing various activities. This will give a better response because they are not being asked to brag or judge the quality of their work. Usually, if someone enjoys doing something, they have relative skill at it. You can also ask people what skill they would like to further develop. This would provide some guidance as to where people would like to participate.

If you run into reluctance when trying to enlist needed help, try to discover what is at the heart of the problem. Some people are just shy and need to be asked. Some people are afraid to commit to a nebulous project that they are not sure they can handle. Therefore make sure to show people exactly what their responsibilities will be. When people know specifically what is expected, they are more willing to become involved.

Another way to handle reluctance is to ask someone to do a *small* job and gauge that person's response. Sometimes it is the pressure of the commitment that sends people running. Therefore lighten the pressure situation. If a person responds positively, give him or her a bigger chunk of work next time. For example, a person may turn down cutting out 100 name tags but say yes to doing 10.

This method of doling out work in smaller quantities is also valuable in developing new or untried help. You can gauge by the results whether you have placed a person in a job for which he or she is gifted or whether you need to direct that person to some other area. Since you have only given this person a few items to do, you are not jeopardizing the event.

Recruiting can be difficult but it is also very rewarding to have a part in developing people and helping them to stretch and grow to the glory of God. After all, isn't that what ministering is all about?

Learning to Accept Praise
A simple thanks is appropriate when given a compliment about the event. These encouragements are to be savored and enjoyed. The Lord has used you in a significant way in someone's life. Rejoice! Do not in false humility speak poorly of the event or pick out its flaws. People will find enough wrong with even the most perfect event; you do not have to help them. Be thankful for the success God has given and do not slap Him in the face by saying that His blessing was not enough.

Another acceptable response is to enthusiastically say, "Yes, didn't this turn out great? The Lord is so good!" or "Yes, I really appreciated the speaker!" or "This was great fun!" These responses help you verbally disassociate yourself with the event and redirect the praise to the Lord and others.

It is important, also, that you pass along the credit not only to the Lord but also to the many others who had a part in it. This encourages others and gives them confidence. It is part of contributing to their successful experience. The more credit you pass on, the less intimidated people will be of you. The Lord knows what ideas were yours and what you did. Let that be enough. Look at it as storing up secret treasure in heaven.

Don't forget to write short notes of thanks to those involved. This can be very encouraging and positive feedback can give people the courage to bite off a bigger piece next time. Remember that we are being Christlike when we express our gratitude to those who have labored with us. And don't forget to send a hardy thank-you heavenward to the One from whom the blessing came in the first place.

THREE

Developing
Creative Ideas

So how do you go about planning a special event? First, bathe it in prayer. Meaningful success comes only from the Lord, so pray to Him and ask Him for it. The Lord is the Great Creator; ask Him for creative ideas and the ability to see and solve problems before they become crisis situations. Ask the Lord for sensitivity to others and also ask that people will be built up. Pray that the Lord will bless the event and that it will accomplish His goals.

Second, set goals. It is important to have clearly in mind what you are trying to accomplish. Are you trying to reach the lost? Are you trying to build some church unity? Have you reached a milestone that you want to draw people's attention to so that they can rejoice and worship God?

After establishing your goals, choose the type of event and the theme that is most suited to your message. For example, if your purpose is to teach people how to evangelize, then you might choose a workshop format with a gardening theme. This theme could promote the concepts of cultivating relationships, sowing seed, and harvesting. The workshop or seminar format would work well by having people break down into smaller groups for instruction.

There are many types of events from which to choose, each with its own set of problems and benefits. Different types of events are suited to various goals. Choose the type of event that is conducive to what needs to be accomplished.

Types of Events
(This is by no means an exhaustive list)

Banquet	Picnic/cook-out
Dinner	Retreat
Tea	Camp-out
Luncheon	Slumber party
Reception	Seminar
Brunch	Anniversary party
Holiday/Seasonal party	Concert
Baby shower	Film night
Wedding shower	Car rally
Retirement party	Fair
Birthday party	Get-together
Cookie exchange	House raising
Taffy pull	Leaf and rake shake
Convention	Workshop
Program	Singspiration

Decide on the *basics:* the time, the place, and the date. An event can be held at a person's home, at the church fellowship hall, at a restaurant, or in the great outdoors. Make sure to check with the church organizational calendar to avoid conflicting events. If your event is going to be held in a public place, send out scouting parties to various locations to check cleanliness and prices. (Start this process early enough to secure the date you want.)

Developing a Theme
Not every event needs to be thematic in nature, but most functions could be improved by a theme. A theme helps focus attention on the main topic. It provides a unifying factor that pulls the event together, preventing an affair from looking disjointed. When planning thematically, all areas of the event — the publicity, registration, food, decorations, and agenda — will reinforce each other. This tends to drive the message home.

When choosing a theme the possibilities are endless. There are many sources from which to draw ideas. Themes can be gathered from Bible verses, especially those with word pictures. They can be built around songs, poems, fables, stories, historical eras, or foreign countries. These international themes are especially adaptable for a missions banquet. Occupations, like nursing or construction, can be used to create themes. Also modes of transportation such as trucks, trains, boats, planes, and bikes can be utilized especially for an event that involves men and boys.

People expect certain motifs for Christmas, Valentines' Day, as well as the other holidays. Therefore, the trick in choosing these themes is to find creative variations of prescribed motifs. For instance when planning a Christmas banquet, try using angels one year, bells the next, and sleds the third year. All the banquets would be "Christmasy" yet different in focus.

Household items can also be used to get ideas — teacups, aprons, hats, and hammers to name just a few. Extract a message from the function of these items to teach a spiritual lesson. Aprons could denote service and lessons on friendship could be derived from teacups.

Nature has a wellspring of ideas that can be worked into banquets or other types of special events. Plants, flowers, or trees bring a variety of colors and textures to mind. Animals such as bears, bees, butterflies, or bunnies could be worked into a theme, especially if some research is done to discover interesting habits which can then be applied to spiritual truth. Geographic themes, such as oceans, deserts, and mountains can apply to a variety of messages. Other scientific phenomena, such as space, electricity, and prisms, have not been tapped as much but could be quite interesting and thought provoking.

Another approach in choosing a theme is to borrow somebody's collection and use it for displays or centerpieces. Such collections might include dolls, bells, stamps, and so forth.

Another easy way to choose a theme is to shop for the paper plates and napkins first. Build the theme of the event around the picture or print on the plate. This gives the event a natural tie-in with the decorations. This works great with birthdays, showers, and anniversaries. It would also work well with seasonal parties.

A preschool coloring book can provide another resource both for getting an idea for a theme, and for patterns to use in the decorations.

One caution here: don't repeat themes frequently. The

themes of successive events need to be different. It's hard to plan the next affair after a very successful event because of people's natural tendency to compare. Many times the second or simpler event suffers in the judging. The best way to solve this problem is to make sure the next banquet is very different and not give in to the temptation to think, "It worked before; let's do it again."

Other Creative Elements

Motif. Motif is the *visual* representation of the theme. Often the motif and theme will work out to be the same. For instance, with a "hat" theme, the visual symbol obviously is hats. In an event that uses a more abstract theme such as "God's Promises," one might use a rainbow as the motif (recalling the Lord's sign to Noah after the Flood). The motif can consist of one main symbol that is repeated to bring unity to the event. A country theme might choose a house, heart, or goose as the main symbol. This symbol can be used on publicity posters, programs, invitations, and the like. Or a motif can consist of a group of symbols that are components of the theme. A banquet with a sewing theme might use buttons, spools, tape measures, patterns, and sewing machines to visually represent the theme.

To develop the motif, brainstorm to compile a list of words that relate to the theme. For example, an Indian theme could end up with a pool of motif words that read like this: wampum, baskets, tepee, totem pole, buffalo, moccasins, feathers, bow and arrows, tomahawk, fringes, war paint, and canoes. This list of words is vitally important because it is used to stimulate ideas that can be applied to all areas of the event. Tepees can be set up to house the registration. Centerpieces can be fashioned to look like totem poles. Nut cups can be made to resemble moccasins or baskets. Indian blankets and designs can be placed on the walls.

Mood. Using the list of motif words, decide what mood or atmosphere these words suggest. Make sure this mood will work with the goals. Write down any words that portray this mood. Is the event going to be bright, cheerful, and happy, or bold, crisp, and direct? Think in terms of mass. Some themes are heavy with velvet or brocade. A medieval banquet could be done in rich heavy drapes and colors. The lettering on the programs would be Gothic. A winter banquet with soft paper snowflakes moving gently overhead with scores of trees grouped to look like a forest is light and airy. You would need white table cloths to keep it light; red ones would weigh it down visually. It is important that the feel and mood be uniform throughout.

As with the theme, try to make the mood for this event different from the preceding event. If one event was elegant, make the next one cute or funny. If one event was soft with pastels, make the next bright and bold. This distracts people from comparing.

Color. Next choose a color scheme that would best portray the mood and the theme. A sewing theme thrives with small calico prints. Pastels do well with flowers and spring. Bold primary colors go well with circus themes or a bright Mexican fiesta. Colors make a big impact on the event so it is wise to choose the ones that are most effective with the theme.

Message. Deciding on the message or key idea that is to be communicated is crucial. This is where the imparting of spiritual truth takes place. Ideally it is best to coordinate the message with the theme. A sewing theme might discuss how Jesus is our pattern for living. A gardening theme might encourage people to plant godly seeds in their hearts so that their lives can be fruitful. A nautical theme might challenge those attending to let Christ be captain of their lives.

Title. The best titles are those that combine the theme and give a glimmer of the key idea. Titles can be useful to label the event for publicity's benefit and can contribute to the building of anticipation.

Texture. Incorporate a variety of textures that are appropriate for the theme. Textures make things look and feel interesting. They break up the monotony. Textures amplify the atmosphere that is being created. Does the event lend itself to rough gnarled wood as in a pioneer theme? A Japanese theme would welcome the sheen of satin and silk with the parchment feel of rice paper. An ocean theme would be enhanced by gritty sand and smooth shells. A homespun country brunch suggests cotton. Contrasting textures can be used as long as they are complementary and mesh with the theme.

Mesh. A special event is most effective when all areas reinforce each other. Just as a magnifying glass focuses scattered light to a central point, so careful planning uses color, theme, and mood to communicate the message to the mind, the emotions, and the spirit. The harmonious fitting together of all the pieces of an event is called mesh.

Apply the theme, mood, color, texture, and message to all areas of the event. The publicity committee now knows what colors to use on the posters and what types of pictures and symbols would be appropriate. The registration committee can use the list of motif words to come up with display items for the sign-up table. The decorations committee can use the motif words to come up with creative ideas for name tags, favors, and nut cups. The food committee can decide if a certain menu would enhance the theme and can color coordinate the food and drinks. The agenda committee follows the theme in their choice of skits, poems, and activities — thus intensifying the impact of the message. Consider the following example. A homespun theme with gingham, calico, and antiques suggests small table groupings and family-style service. Homemade bread and vegetable soup would reinforce the cozy atmosphere. Waitresses in long dresses with crisp white aprons could serve applesauce in big wooden bowls while a barbershop quartet sings turn of the century music. A dramatic narrative done in the first person of some great man of God from that time period could contribute to an unforgettable evening. Each element helps to increase the effectiveness of the others. Many strands make a beautiful tapestry just as the careful weaving of mood and theme throughout an affair produces a superlative event.

If each committee applies the theme to its area, the job will be easier for everyone. The decorations provide the backdrop for the skits and message. Color coordinated punch and a thematically decorated cake can contribute to the decorations.

Think in terms of shape and dimension when trying to come up with creative applications. Sometimes name tags and posters can be made three-dimensional. Thematic words that suggest a low bowl shape can be turned into nut cups. Place mats, name tags, and posters can be cut in the shape of a motif. Fabric and lace can add texture to a program.

To help you with your planning, this chapter concludes with a variety of themes and their accompanying titles and motif words. Let them be a springboard for your own creative touch.

Theme List

Theme	Title	Motif Words
Gems	Gems for His Crown	tiara, crown, ruby, King, emerald, diamond
Underwater	Exploring Davy Jones' Locker	seaweed, shells, sand, fish, shipwrecks
Pirates	Treasure at Pirate's Cove	treasure chest, jewels, map, ship, Jolly Rogers
Sports	Winning at the Game of Life	hurdles, soccer, referees, whistles, footballs
Texas	Deep in the Heart of Texas	cowboys, cactus, oil wells, yellow rose
Gold Prospecting	Prospecting at Paradise Mine	pick, shovel, donkey, mine, tin plates, lanterns
Political Convention	Election Day Dinner	flags, straw hats, campaign buttons, stars
Lawyers	Day in Court	hammer, judge, jail, witness, trial, jury
Picnic	Picnic in the Park	red gingham, ants, baskets, watermelon, races
Fishing	Fishing for Men	fishing pole, bait, boat, pond, trout, flies
International	Jesus Loves the Little Children	international costumes, travel posters, globes
Tools	Nuts and Bolts	tool box, hammer, ruler, saw, nails
Greece	An Afternoon in Ancient Athens	togas, pillars, marble, mythology, urns, fountains
Sewing	Patterns for Living	needle, thread, fabric, pattern, pin cushion
Military	Onward Christian Soldiers	helmet, uniform, medals, boots, tanks, camouflage
Olympics	Going for the Gold	laurel leaves, torch, races, Olympic emblem
Circus	Under the Big Top	clowns, tents, elephants, tightrope, trapeze
Clocks	Sands of Time	hour glass, clock faces, gears, grandfather clocks
Indians	Indian Pow-Wow	canoe, wampum, tepee, totem pole, feathers
Fruit	Fruit of the Spirit	grapes, apples, arbors, vines, fruit bowls
Bees	Busy Bee Brunch	hive, queen bee, flowers, stinger, honey
Dolls	Ladies' Doll House Luncheon	doll house, Raggedy Ann, china dolls, canopy bed
World	Around the World in 80 Minutes	globe, hot air balloons, travel posters, clocks
Teacup	Tea for Two	china, flowers, silver, tea kettles
Ducks	Duck Hunting Dinner	mallards, cattails, retriever dogs, pond

Theme	Title	Motif Words
Farm	Grandma's Farm	sheep, cows, goats, hay, pigs, barn, chickens
Hawaii	A Hawaiian Luau	grass skirts, fire, coconut, lei
Japan	Japanese Garden Tea	kimono, chopsticks, fan, oriental flower, pagoda
Mexico	A Mexican Fiesta	sombrero, burro, bull fight, poncho, bandito
Germany	Castles on the Rhine	barons, tuba, sausages, dirndls, strudel, mugs
Holland	Dutch Treat	windmill, wooden shoes, dikes, tulips, Dutch hats
Arabia	Arabian Nights	tents, camels, harems, veils, oriental rugs
Ireland	Pot o' Gold Potluck	green, shamrocks, leprechaun, rainbow, pot of gold
China	China Town Chow Down	dragons, rickshaws, pigtails, chopsticks, pagoda
Australia	A Day Down Under	kangaroos, koala bears, Aussie hats, aborigines
Jungle	A Jungle Safari	lions, huts, warriors, spears, monkeys, palm trees
France	April in Paris	Eiffel tower, Triumphal arch, artists, cafés
Nautical	Rescue the Perishing	lighthouse, life preserver, rocks, waves, ships
Wagon Train	Westward Ho	covered wagons, buffalo, Indians, camp fire, oxen
Old West	The Taming of the West	guns, cowboy hats, horses, sheriff, outlaws, lasso
Universe	Out of This World Banquet	sun, planets, stars, space, space ships, Martians
Aprons	Service with a Smile	aprons all types
Spring Rain	April Showers Brunch	raindrops, clouds, umbrellas, rain coats
Wishes	Wishing Well Luncheon	stone well, flowers, coins
Meadow	Ladies' Lady Bug Luncheon	ladybugs, birds, caterpillars, leaves, nests
Beach	Soaking in the Sonshine	sand, sunglasses, umbrella, pail, shovel, towels
Apples	Apple Harvest Festival	apples, barrels, trees, applesauce, pies
Pumpkin	Pumpkin Party	pumpkins, pumpkin patch, squash, pies, cornucopia
Leaves	Come Little Leaves Luncheon	leaves, trees, wind, rake, basket, bulbs, mums
Pilgrim	Thanksgiving Dinner	pilgrims, Indians, thatch huts, Mayflower
Winter	Winter Wonderland Banquet	snowflakes, snowmen, skates, icicles, mittens
Eskimos	Land of the Midnight Sun	igloo, dogsled, ivory, parka, kayak, seals, snow
Trucks	Keep on Truck'n	truck stop, coffee mug, semi, dump trucks, diesel

Theme	Title	Motif Words
Ships	Ship Shape Supper	barges, tug boats, captain hats, ocean liners
Planes	Flying High with the Lord	planes, scarf, goggles, airport, radio, air sock
Trains	The Heaven Express	tracks, railroad crossing signs, engineer hat
Football	Touch Down Dinner	football, field, helmet, chalkboard, cheerleaders
Baseball	Seventh Inning Outing	pennant, hot dogs, cap, ball, bat, glove, umpire
Art	The Masterpiece	paint, brushes, paint cans, splatters, paint shirt
Chickens	Country Chicken Breakfast	coop, chicken wire, rooster, eggs, feathers
Bride	Wedding Day Delights	wedding gown, flowers, ring, doves, hearts, veil
Heaven	Pearly Gates Banquet	clouds, harp, angels, gold, pearly gates, halo
Architecture	Blueprints for Living	houses, blueprints, house plans, hammer, nails

FOUR

Getting Organized

There are several methods of organizing an event. Much depends on the size of the event. Showers, birthday parties, and many simple get-togethers can easily be done by one to three people. Planning these simple events provides great opportunities to build one-on-one relationships. Just make sure to divide up the tasks and check on one another. Small events are just as susceptible to the "pitfalls" as large ones.

For large events you need a framework that divides the workload. The model I find most helpful is the delegated committee system, where the coordinator directs five to six committees (possibly seven if you need child care). Too many committees can become cumbersome when trying to find a time when everyone can get together, but five to six is workable. These committees are publicity, registration, decorations, refreshments, agenda, and cleanup:

- The *publicity committee* takes care of all posters, bulletin announcements, invitations, and anything else that promotes the event.
- The *registration committee* takes care of signing up people, collecting money for tickets, distributing name tags, keeping track of names and addresses, etc.
- The *decorations committee* creates the atmosphere and is responsible for how the event looks. I usually place paper goods here rather than with the food, unless the event (like a picnic) doesn't require much in the way of decorations.

32

- The *refreshment committee* plans the menu and makes sure that the food is there in sufficient quantities.
- The *agenda committee* oversees anything that is going to happen at the event — special music, choosing an emcee, getting the sound system working, assigning a skit, etc.
- The *cleanup committee* is responsible for making sure that everything gets put back in place. Sometimes this committee can be absorbed into the others if each committee cleans up after itself. I find that it is valuable to incorporate new help here because many people burn out after the event when their adrenaline has quit pumping, especially the decorations and food people.

Other committees or subcommittees can be formed if an event calls for a particular need but these five or six are the main ones.

Another way of organizing an event is the coordinator-directed method. This system breaks down all tasks in bite-sized pieces and enlists people directly, bypassing the committee head positions altogether. This system works very efficiently for simple events because there is only one leader. The communication network is not nearly so complicated. This approach is helpful if no one is willing to take responsibility to lead a department. It also allows the coordinator to retain creative control over the event. There are, however, disadvantages to this approach. For one thing, it takes more work to oversee the details because, in effect, the coordinator becomes the chairman of all the committees. The other disadvantage to this system is that it is not as conducive to developing leadership as the delegated committee system. A lot depends on the personality of the coordinator, the character of the people, and the tradition of the church.

How to Use Worksheets

It has been my experience that whenever people have taken on the responsibility of doing a special event, they inevitably sit down with a blank piece of paper and say, "Let's see, what do we need? Plates, napkins, maybe we can get Mr. So-and-So to speak . . . ummm, what else?" They rethink the same list over and over, reinventing the wheel. Add to this the vague uneasy feeling that they know they are forgetting something but for the life of them, they can't remember what it is!

One way to combat this problem is to use worksheets which can act as memory prompters. All you have to do is fill in the blanks. Fill in the colors and quantities of items. Record the name and phone numbers of personnel so that the information you need is at your fingertips. These worksheets also help to crystallize who is doing what. The committee personnel pages also enable the committee heads to know who to go to for the information that they need. Cross out the options that are not useful for your particular event. You may still feel like you are forgetting something, but you can rest assured knowing that the major areas are covered.

A Simple 6-Step System

So exactly how do we go about organizing an event? Six basic steps will get us from here to there.

Step one: Pray

Step two: Decide on organizational system:
- simple (one or two people running event)
- delegated-committee (committees overseen by coordinator)
- coordinator-directed (event chopped up into bite-sized tasks)

Step three: Worksheets (Copy, enlarge, adapt, fill in)
- Choose appropriate worksheets
  - Simple & coordinator directed events will need worksheets #1–6, located at the end of this chapter.
  - Committe run events will need the following:
    Coordinator: Worksheets 1–6, 22 located in this chapter
    Publicity: Worksheets 7–10, located in chapter 6
    Registration: Worksheets 11–12, located in chapter 7
    Decorations: Worksheets 13–15, located in chapter 8
    Refreshments: Worksheets 16–17, located in chapter 9
    Agenda: Worksheets 18–19, located in chapter 10
    Child Care: Worksheet 20, located in chapter 11
    Clean-up: Worksheet 21, located in chapter 11
    Finances: Worksheets 22–23, located in chapter 11
- Put worksheets in a pocketed folder. Use clasp envelope to centralize receipts.
- Use worksheets to:
  - Figure out basics (when, where, type of event; secure place early; clear date with church calendar)
  - Crystallize goals

— Choose theme
— Compile motif words (see chapter 3)
— Decide color scheme and mood
— Formulate thrust/message
— Compose title
— Flesh out event (see chapter 3)
  Apply theme to details of event
  Use motif words for ideas

Step four: Check periodically on committee heads (encourage and rescue if needed)

Step five: Day of Event
● Arrive early
● Be preapred to troubleshoot
● Jump in and help if committee head looks taxed

Step six: After Event
● Thank the Lord
● Provide report to the church
● Square finances

WORKSHEET 1

The Special Event Planner

Event:	Date:
Audience:	Time:
Projected Attendance:	Place:
Actual Attendance:	Dress:

Goal: *(circle appropriate choices)*

Instruction	Celebration	Honor
Evangelism	Recreation	Fellowship
Worship	Fund-raising	Other

Theme:

Color:

Mood:

Motif:

Message: Attractions:

Title: Bring:

Committees	Name	Phone

Coordinator:
Publicity:
Registration:
Decorations:
Refreshments:
Agenda:
  Music Coordinator:
  Emcee:
  Sound/Light man:
  Greeter:
  Speaker/Group:
Child care:
Clean-up:
Finances:

WORKSHEET 2

Overview of Publicity and Registration

Publicity: Post dates:

Announcement ideas: Flyers/invitations:

Bulletin board/poster ideas: Displays:

Registration: Registration dates:

Table decorations: Name tags:

Sign-up sheet/poster:

WORKSHEET 3

Overview of Decorations

Outdoor entrance: Foyer:

Walls: Windows:

Ceiling: Floors:

Stage/front: Buffet table:

Tablecloth/place mats: Plates/napkins:

Flatware: Place cards:

Cups: Nut cups/favors:

Programs: Centerpieces:

WORKSHEET 4

Overview of Room Arrangement

Setup date: Setup time:
Projected attendance: Tables needed:

(Sketch placement of tables, serving tables, props, etc.)

WORKSHEET 5

Overview of Refreshments

Menu: Drinks: Coffee
                                                        Tea
                                                        Punch
                                                        Soda

Style of service: *(circle choice)*
  Buffet   Served   Hostess   Other:

Method of acquiring food: *(circle choice)*
  Open potluck   Assigned potluck
  Committee catered   Professionally catered

Condiments needed: *(check choices)*
  Cream   Butter   Catsup   Other:
  Sugar   Salt/Pepper   Mustard

Food layout plan for buffet table:

Equipment needed:

WORKSHEET 6

Overview of Agenda

Activities:

Music:
  Background music:
  Special music:

Schedule:

Time	Activity	Personnel	Duration

FIVE
The
Coordinator

The coordinator's job is a very demanding one, heavy with responsibility. You must plan and execute an event with a myriad of details. You must minister to your team so that all members feel successful at accomplishing their tasks. Though this is a taxing job, it can be tremendously rewarding to see ideas come to life and people blessed.

The coordinator is responsible to recruit committee heads and to funnel to them as much help as possible. He or she needs to *delegate* duties rather than actually do all the legwork alone. A coordinator who does not learn to commission others will become overwhelmed quickly and the events will not reach their potential.

The coordinator oversees the event, making sure that all is progressing on schedule. The coordinator must check and make sure that the plans of the committees mesh. For example, he or she must be aware of how much room the agenda people need to do their skit and convey this information to the decorations people. The coordinator is the communication center and needs to keep abreast of current information in order to give accurate answers to questions. It is of utmost importance that the coordinator keep up on details of the event because this person sees the overall picture. For the coordinator there should be no surprises; good planning should ensure that all facets of the event will work together.

Do not be afraid to plan a more involved event. Many times it is more rewarding to do extra than just the minimum. To make dinner is work, to make a Thanksgiving feast is much more work but definitely more enjoyable. The same principle holds true for special events.

A wise coordinator will encourage the committee heads by being enthusiastically interested in the details of their plans. Praising their accomplishments and admiring their work will give the committee heads a morale boost as well as confidence. This type of encouragement develops a team mentality.

Leading the Leaders

Though a coordinator must know what is going on in each committee, it is important to let the committee leaders do things their own way. Resist the urge to micro-manage. This may mean sacrificing ideas so that the committee heads can institute some of their own brainchilds. It may be hard for a coordinator to do, but without such freedom creativity will be stifled. You do not want the committee heads to become glorified "go-fers" and the coordinator a prima donna. This will cause resentment and friction. You must be available to gently guide without taking over and being pushy.

Sometimes committee heads are uncomfortable with the pre-scribed ideas. The ideas can seem too radical or too conservative, making committee heads uneasy. One idea may work well for a person with a flamboyant personality but that idea given to a quieter person may be quite threatening. Sometimes an idea can seem too conservative. Creative people may view it as boring and hesitate to put their names and endorsements on such a plan. This is why the coordinator should offer a variety of suggestions and then give the committee heads some leeway to do their job in a way that is best suited to their personalities.

Enthusiasm is a fragile thing that can easily be extinguished. People, especially creative ones, get most excited over their own ideas. If you squelch their ideas, you may find that you have thrown water on the fires of excitement for the whole project. You do not want to be perceived as a dictator in search of slaves. Generally speaking if you are receptive to the ideas of others, they will be receptive to yours.

The guideline is to allow other ideas to become operative as long as they do not destroy the basic theme. This may mean

43

allowing good ideas to replace great ones as long as the theme identity remains intact. Sensitivity is the key word here. There is a verse in Romans 12:18 that states: "as much as is within you live at peace with all men." Paraphrased and adapted, this principle could be restated, "As much as lies within you, allow others to express themselves and develop." Here is an area to "esteem others [and their ideas] as more important than yourself."

Be Careful with Criticism

Make sure before giving negative input that it is really necessary. Is the criticism worth the stress on the relationship? So what if the punch isn't the right color? Sure, it would have looked better if it matched, but in scope of time and eternity, who cares? It is certainly not worth discouraging the saints. I know of a girl who was once raked over the coals for leaving a spoon in the sink. This is not necessary!

If a word of reproof *must* be spoken or an idea must be rejected, do it tactfully and gently. Try approaching the situation from a "we" perspective. You will meet with more success if you say, "What should we do with all these extra plates? Is there any way we can take them back?" rather than saying, "Why did you buy so many extra plates? The church can't afford this extra expense. Next time don't be so extravagant." Stirring in the element of humor can also do much to diffuse the tension of the mistake.

Problems can be addressed during the *evaluation* after the event. Ask committee members what areas were rough and what they could suggest to make them smoother. At this point statements like, "We should really check and make sure all the silverware gets put away" are not so threatening. Try posing problems in questions. "Was there enough food?" "What did we run short on?" "How did we get so far off count?" When posed in this fashion, people do not get defensive because fingers are not being pointed their way. The blame, if any, is shared. Your purpose is not to find the guilty party but rather to solve the problem so that it doesn't happen again. It is much better to have people critique themselves than for you to sit in judgment on them.

Sometimes sandwiching correction between words of praise

works. For example, "I appreciate the work you have done. The posters look great! We really could use a sign-up sheet in operation by next week. Can you take care of that or would you like me to give you a hand?" Make sure that the praise part of the sandwich is genuine.

Of course, if the only time people receive praise from you is as a prelude to criticism, they might get allergic to your compliments. A sympathetic attitude, a noncritical tone of voice, and gentle eyes go a long way in cradling people's emotions while still getting the job done.

Ideally the coordinator should have tasks delegated and information given out well before the time of the event. This frees up the coordinator to deal with any last minute disasters that might crop up. As a coordinator you are successful when the event you have planned can run by itself.

A coordinator must realize that putting on the event is only half of the job. The other half is developing people. No matter how beautiful the event is, it is not a complete success if division and strife have run rampant. Never forget that *people are more important than the event.*

Even if everything does not turn out just right, if your people have been given the opportunity to expand in a loving and nonthreatening environment, you are still successful. The kingdom of God is made up of people, not nut cups.

The Assistant Coordinator
Most of the time, especially if the event is at all complex, it is a good idea to enlist an *assistant coordinator*. This person can be a coordinator's right hand. The assistant can aid with the multitude of errands, and phone calls, and general legwork. This person can be assigned to work with a particular committee that needs direction or has an extensive job. The assistant should be knowledgeable enough about the whole event to act as the coordinator's substitute if necessary. The assistant can also help the coordinator spot areas that need attention and assist in the rescuing process.

Having an assistant is a marvelous way to train someone how to do an event. It is a nonthreatening way of building confidence. The assistant takes part in all areas but is under supervision. After someone assists for a while, that person will have the

45

ability and the confidence to put together a whole event.

One word of caution: though it sounds terribly undemo-cratic, have only one person ultimately responsible. Someone needs to be accountable. Otherwise the coordinators may make decisions in conflict with each other, or they may be paraylzed to make any decision at all until they can get each other's agreement. This can make organizing an event needlessly com-plicated and create an atmosphere of uncertainty for all concerned.

SIX

Publicity

Publicity is vitally important. If interest is not sparked and people do not come, your event is in vain. Since most people normally end up doing what they *want* to do, the publicity for a special event should motivate people to *want* to come. Publicity must stimulate enough interest to overcome inertia. After a long day it is easier to collapse on the couch with a soda and the TV remote control, than to get dressed and go out. Publicity needs to give people the push to overcome this tendency by conveying that this is a special event which no one will want to miss.

The publicity committee must also communicate the necessary information: who, what, when, where, and why. Because most people do not remember details the first time they hear them, publicity should provide repeated reminders about the event.

Encourage the publicity committee to see that all posters, bulletin boards, and other visuals mesh with the event's theme. And they should make sure the spelling is correct; spelling errors give the impression of carelessness — an impression which might rub off on the event itself.

Publicity Options
Personal verbal invitations. Nothing takes the place of having people personally invite others to events. This is the single most important method of publicity. When people realize they are wanted — personally — they are more likely to attend. Personal

invitations give folks the feeling that they will know someone at the event, that they are accepted. All committee heads should be encouraged to invite people personally and should urge their helpers to do the same.

Church bulletin. An announcement should be placed in the bulletin four to six weeks ahead of time depending on the size of the event. Include the name and phone number of the coordinator or the publicity chairman so that people know who to contact for more information.

Invitations. Invitations can stimulate interest in an event. They have two purposes: reminder cards for the congregation, and a card for people to use when inviting their friends to the event. The publicity committee is responsible for designing and producing invitations. They could be placed on the registration table so that people could pick them up to use to invite friends. They could be given out personally or mailed. The person producing invitations should work closely with the decoration committee so the invitations complement the decorations. Many times the same artist or artwork can be used.

Flyers. Flyers are slips of paper that present information in an exciting way. Flyers can be sent in the mail, slipped in the church bulletin, or given out by hand. These work well for an evangelistic campaign, daily Vacation Bible School, Bible clubs, fairs—anything where the general public is encouraged to come.

Posters. Posters are a great publicity option because they are very versatile and can be put up and taken down easily. Posters should be placed in high traffic areas: halls, lobbies, washrooms, and so forth. When choosing a spot, look for a focal point—the space directly opposite the entrance door, the wall across the way from the washroom, wherever the eye naturally falls. Posters should be put in place three to four weeks before the event.

Posters can be created in all shapes and sizes. Having several people create posters allows for a wide variety of styles and ideas. Make sure that the basic information is given out to the people in charge of producing the poster, including the color and theme. Poster contests can help stimulate involvement, communicate the information, and provide a large quantity of posters for decoration or for advertisement.

Bulletin boards. Bulletin board displays are also quite useful in promoting your event. The background can be composed of wrapping paper, large pieces of construction paper, or a big remnant of cloth. Cloth, cotton, foil, silk flowers, sandpaper, etc., can add texture. Three-dimensional objects such as rag dolls or artifacts from various countries can be attached with long hat pins. When asking someone to make a bulletin board display, the leader should include some initial seed ideas or rough drawings to stimulate thought. Allow the person freedom, however, to be creative and come up with his or her own ideas.

Specify the size of the board when giving your helpers the assignment. This aids them in decisions concerning the size of the lettering and the placement of items. The designer can then lay out the design and see if it fits in the allotted space—passing his approval in the privacy of his own home. If the board doesn't work, adjustments can be made without an audience.

Displays. A display is a three-dimensional grouping of objects used to create interest. This is a very creative approach to publicizing an event. If the theme revolved around sewing, for example, one could place a sewing form in the foyer with pieces of information pinned to it. A nautical theme might be promoted by hanging a life-saving ring on the wall. A country theme might use quilts, an old rocker, and a butter churn.

Live announcements. Live announcements can be as simple as the pastor announcing the event on Sunday morning, or they can be very creative—perhaps using skits or costuming. We once had our pastor unpack a picnic basket from the pulpit to announce what to bring to the picnic. Everyone leaving the sanctuary that day knew that a picnic was coming up! People will not remember the event if it has only been announced once. That is why it is good to have the event announced in small and large meetings.

Memos. A short memo is used to give the basic facts to people who need to know the details. Send out memos to the leadership of the church—such as pastors, deacons, and elders—so that they are well-informed. Use memos for the people who are responsible for making announcements to each group in the church.

Phone calling. Another method of publicizing an event is to use the phone, calling everyone in the church directory or blanketing a certain area. This task is easiest to accomplish when split up among several people. Make sure to coordinate this with the registration committee in case there is important data to collect. It would be a waste of precious time and talent to have both committees calling the same list.

Radio/TV spots. Use radio and/or TV spots only if the event is intended to minister to the outside community. Many stations have community bulletin board features which are free or have a minimal fee. Generally the information needs to be broadcast one to two weeks in advance.

Signs. Signs in front of the church can be an effective means of communicating. They can be used for special church meetings, concerts, Vacation Bible School, etc. It is important that people know that *this* is the spot where the activity is being held. Signs can have a subtle effect on the community, in that the community sees that something is going on. This might later influence people to visit. Of course this method pales in effectiveness when compared to examples of enthusiastic, righteous testimonies of God's people, but nonetheless every little bit helps. The sign should be put up one to two weeks prior to the event.

Newsletters/Newspapers. Short, interesting articles could be written to report on a given activity. A press release to a local newspaper could be utilized to publicize events designed for outreach in the community. A press release would contain the basic information relating to the event: who, what, where, when, why, and how much.

WORKSHEET 7

Personnel Worksheet: Publicity

Event: Theme:

Audience: Title:

Date: Goal:

Time: Message:

Place: Color:

Cost: Mood:

Projected attendance: Motif:

Publicity budget: Attractions:

Dress: Bring:

Committees	Name	Phone
Coordinator:		
Registration:		
Decorations:		
Refreshments:		
Agenda:		
Clean-up:		
Child care:		
Other:		
Publicity:		
Post dates:		
Helpers:		

WORKSHEET 8

Publicity Worksheet

Options of Medium: (check appropriate options)

☐ **Flyers:**
When to be distributed:
Where to be distributed:

☐ **Memos to Leadership:**
When to be distributed:

☐ **Invitations:**
When to be distributed:
Where to distribute:

☐ **Phone Calling:**
When to call:
Who to call:

☐ **Posters:**
When to be posted:
Where to be posted:

☐ **Radio:**
When to broadcast:
Which station:

☐ **Bulletin Boards:**
When to be displayed:
Where to be displayed:

☐ **Newspaper Ad:**
When to run:
Which newspaper:

☐ **Displays:**
When to be set up:
Where to be set up:

☐ **TV Spot:**
When to broadcast:
Which station:

☐ **Verbal Invitations:**
Strategy:

☐ **Outdoor Sign:**
When to be set up:
Design ideas:

☐ **Church Bulletin:**
When to be posted:
Announcement draft:

☐ **Live Announcements:**
When to be announced:
Where/how:

☐ **Newsletter Article:**
When to run:

☐ **Press Release:**
When to run:

WORKSHEET 9

Publicity: Bulletin Boards/Posters

Event information:

Event:
Date:
Place:
Cost:
Dress:
Bring:

Personnel:

Event title:
Time:
Audience:
Baby-sitting:
Attractions:

Technical information:

Theme:
Message:
Mood:
Size of board: _____ x _____
Date needed for posting:

Goal:
Color:
Motif:
Location of board:

Design ideas:

WORKSHEET 10

Memo

MEMO

To:
From:
Message: When to post or publicize:

Event information:
Event: Date:
Event title: Attractions:
Place: Time:
Cost: Baby-sitting:
For: Bring:
Dress: Other:

SEVEN

Registration

It is the job of the registration committee to get a relatively accurate count of how many people plan to attend an event. The registration committee also aids the publicity committee in building anticipation for the event, and is responsible for collecting important data. It can ascertain the need for child care. It can delegate who is to bring what dish to a potluck. It can also be involved with the collection of money if tickets are to be sold or if money is to be collected.

Having people sign up prior to the event is valuable because this encourages people to commit to attend. Somehow, writing their name down on the list helps people to cement the decision. However, the planners should remember to allow easy outs for people who have last minute changes of plans. If people are made to feel guilty or experience heavy pressure, they may not sign up the next time, and you may have lost your chance to minister to that person.

The registration committee is also responsible for taking attendance at the event and giving the count to the coordinator. Keeping a file with names and addresses for follow-up would also be handled by the registration committee. This is not necessary for all events but is helpful in evangelistic endeavors such as Vacation Bible School.

It is important that the registration committee coordinates with the event's theme. The sign-up sheet, the registration table decorations, etc. should mesh, or the impact is diluted. The registration committee shares the responsibility with the publicity committee of giving people their first impression of the event.

Registration Options

There are several convenient ways of registering people. Whatever the method, registration is most effective if headed by an enthusiastic person who is actively encouraging people to sign up. In addition to giving a personal touch, this provides a person who can answer questions such as, "Are guests welcome?" "Are pets allowed on the park grounds?" "What sort of child care will be provided?" An informed registration person can help clarify any misconceptions about the event. For instance, countless women have stayed home from mother-daughter banquets because they did not have a daughter. A registrar could have informed them that this event was intended for all ladies, young and old.

Registration table. A registration table set up in a high-traffic area can be an effective way of registering people. It can include invitations, tickets, the sign-up sheet, and any props, displays, or decorations that would enhance the visual impact. The table should also include information about the event. This can be written in calligraphy and put in a frame or simply written out on the sign-up sheet.

The sign-up poster. For some events a poster that has places for people to sign up may be desirable. This is especially helpful in a foyer that has limited space. Make sure the poster is thematically correct. It should be placed three to four weeks in advance. For best results it should be manned.

The sign-up sheet. The sign-up sheet is the place where people mark their names to show they intend to attend the event. It should reflect the mood, color, and theme of the event. Proper choice of paper can enhance the look. Parchment with charred edges, for instance, can enhance a medieval theme. My favorite standby is card stock, which is sturdy and versatile. It comes in 8½" by 11" size, has the same consistency as index cards, and is available from office supply stores. An imaginative mind could dream up many other creative mediums for the sign-up sheet. Think how interest would be stimulated if guests had to carve their names in wet clay tablets introducing a Babylonian Feast! Hearts made of construction paper can be used on Valentine's

Day. Giant feet could be used to enroll people for a footstep banquet. A Roman centurion can register guests for a Christmas banquet on a long parchment scroll.

It is important for the registration committee to check with the food committee to make sure that all the data needed will be gathered. It is immensely helpful to have people include their phone numbers, especially if the refreshment committee later needs to call them.

A general sign-up sheet is where people just sign their names and phone numbers. This is the method normally used when the meal is being catered and money is being collected. A general sign-up sheet is also helpful for open potluck meals where people are asked to bring a dish. Examples of this might be a Mexican Fiesta where people are asked to bring a Mexican dish, or a salad luncheon, or a reception where only desserts are needed.

Assigned potluck meals can be initiated by creating a sign-up sheet with columns, placing a type of food at the top of each column. Food contributions can also be designated by alphabet. For example if your last name begins with A–G bring a main dish, H–M bring a salad, and so on. A creative approach is to designate food by arbitrary criteria such as hair color, eye color, state of birth, month of birth, etc. It is important to discuss this with the food committee. It is the refreshment committee's decision as to how to acquire the food, but is it the registration committee's job to work up a sign-up sheet that will gather the initial required information.

Responsibilities of the Registration Committee at the Event
The registration name tag table. Some events need to have a registration table set up at the event. This is especially important at conferences and seminars that have workshops, or an event like Vacation Bible School where new children come daily. In this case the registration committee is responsible for channeling people to the proper spots. The registration table becomes the hub of communication and records. The registration table is also a great place to distribute name tags. In some events this is its primary function. The table should be set up at the entrance of the hall or in the foyer. The table should be decorated according to the theme.

Name tags. Since one major purpose of a special event is to help people get acquainted, name tags are helpful. It is hard to ask someone's name if he or she has previously been introduced to you and you have forgotten his or her name. Let's face it, some folks have real trouble keeping names and faces straight. Name tags solve the whole problem.

Name tags present another avenue to express creativity and reinforce the theme. They can be made of construction paper, card stock, or other sturdy material. Name tags can be flat or three-dimensional and can be garnished with wiggle eyes, cloth, rickrack, ribbon, and other material that would add interest and texture.

Name tags can also be used to divide people into groups for games or discussion. This can be accomplished by color coding or numbering them on the back.

Ideally name tags should be prewritten if a large attendance is expected. The name tags can then be laid out alphabetically for easy acquisition. Make sure to provide enough light for people to find their name. The use of the table can be avoided if the name tags are placed at place settings or hung on a bulletin board. Always make sure to have extra tags and cards on hand for unexpected guests. Having name tags prewritten allows the line to move quickly and avoids a bottleneck at the name tag table. A smaller, more casual affair does not require prewritten name tags as long as people have the chance to write out their own tags.

Prewritten name tags also allow someone to creatively express the theme through calligraphy or other fancy lettering. Lettering could also be color coordinated, especially if color plays a big role in the event. Matching the lettering of the name tags with the lettering of the programs gives a pretty effect. Lettering should match the mood of the event if at all possible. A circus theme could use dot lettering. A "Castles on the Rhine" theme might need heavy Gothic print. A floral banquet would be complemented with script. Make sure that the names are big enough so that people can read them without coming up close and peering at the tag.

WORKSHEET 11

Personnel Worksheet: Registration

Event: Theme:
Audience: Title:
Date: Goal:
Time: Message:
Place: Color:
Cost: Mood:
Registration budget: Motif:
Dress: Attractions:
Projected attendance: Bring:
Actual attendance:

Committees	Name	Phone

Coordinator:
Publicity:
Refreshments:
Decorations:
Agenda:
Clean-up:
Child care:
Other:
Registration:
    Personnel:
    Dates of registration:

WORKSHEET 12

Registration

Registration table:

    Table decorations:

    Tickets/admission:

Sign-up sheet/poster:

Name tags:

File of names and addresses: *(optional, choose method to be used if needed for follow-up)*

    1. Index card record
    2. Notebook record
    3. Other:

EIGHT

Decorations

Decorations add pizzazz to your event and turn a common get-together into something special. Touches as simple as matching plates and napkins and a flower centerpiece can transform an event from mundane into a real occasion.

Decorations set the mood and tone of an event. They make it fun and can be a real drawing card. They give people a positive first impression. Remember, people decide in the first few seconds what they think about an event. If their hearts are not captured right away, the agenda committee will have a tougher time in communicating because they will have to overcome some initial resistance.

Good decorations may make a difference in whether or not people will invite their friends to future events. People will not invite skeptical friends to an event they think will look thrown together.

Careless neglect of decorations carries the message, "You are not worth the trouble." We read in Colossians 3:23, "Do all things heartily as unto the Lord." Decorations do not have to be expensive or involved; they can be simple and still have that "special" touch.

Decoration Principles
Focal point. A focal point is a picture, object, or group of objects that create interest and cause your eye to rest on a certain spot. Obviously the main focal point should be where the action or

program takes place, but do not neglect the lesser areas. The side of the hall that people first see should be given preference when it comes to decorating.

Touch of class. These are the "little extras" that show how much thought and care was put into the event. Look for clever or creative ways to flesh out the theme, even in the small details. For example, lightly dust the tables of a Winter Wonderland Banquet with clear glitter, making them twinkle like new fallen snow. Or give out yellow carnations at a sunny spring luncheon. Or disperse decorated bread dough ornaments at a Christmas banquet. Classy touches favorably surprise guests, making them feel welcome, special, and curious about what will happen next.

Creativity. Review the motif word list, where you thought of as many words as possible that correlated with the theme. Can any of those words be applied to decorating features? A nautical theme might have words like: lighthouse, ship, life preserver, rocks, sand, dim lights, nets, lobster traps, anchor, sailor hat, buoy, navigational maps, ship's wheel. From this list you could think to make lighthouses with flashlights or candle bulbs for centerpieces. Programs could be made with sand and shells to add texture. Little ship nut cups with tiny sails sailing on a blue tablecloth would also reinforce the theme. Stack lobster traps for displays. Hang nets on the walls and ceilings. Place red votive candles in baby food jars to imitate the glassy glow of an old lighthouse.

Contrast. Things stand out better if they contrast. White plates on white tablecloths with white programs are not a good choice unless the theme is purity. Therefore, think about the color of the plates when deciding if the programs should be passed out at the door or placed on the plates. Sometimes inserting a colored place mat between the tablecloth and plates can solve a contrast problem. This principle should be considered when putting together displays and other decorations.

Decoration Options
Outside entrance. The outside entrance is the first thing that the visitors see, and creative decorations there can build excitement and anticipation. Luminarias, which consist of votive candles placed in plain paper bags half-filled with sand, can line the

walks with a welcoming glow. Crepe paper, flags, or balloons can decorate a porch. Sentries could guard the door. Banners could be hung. The outside decorations need to be in keeping with the theme, mood, and color of the event.

Foyer. Some fellowship halls have a foyer. This area too could be thematically decorated with a tasteful display. This is an ideal place for a greeter to meet the guests and the registration/name tag table to be located.

Stage/front. The stage or front is generally the focal point of the room. If the hall has no stage or formal front, the "front" can be placed anywhere in the room, although it is generally better if it is not on the same side as the entrance. Latecomers like to sneak in without parading in front of everyone. There should be some sort of treatment to denote that the action takes place here. Simply placing plants around the podium can do the trick. More elaborate backdrops can be created with various furniture and props. The title of the event can be displayed in the front by suspending it from the ceiling or attaching it to the walls. Letters can be painted or drawn or be made of construction paper, thin cork, wood, Styrofoam, or any other light material that will hold its shape.

Walls. Walls may be decorated in many ways. Hang pictures, quilts, posters, murals, or other objects. Paper cutouts may be taped to the walls. In a banquet with a footprint theme, adorn the walls with giant footprints with verses concerning our "walk with God." The Sunday School could make life-sized drawings of children by tracing around them. The children could color and cut themselves out. This could be used as wall decorations at a "Children of the World" mission banquet.

If the room is to be darkened, every wall decoration should be spotlighted. Do not forget to bring plenty of extension cords and duct tape when setting up. Carefully tape all electrical wires and cords to prevent tripping. Flashlights, floodlights, and desk lamps can be used for this purpose. Place the light in such a way that the light fixture is hidden or unobtrusive. The idea is to draw the eye to the decoration, not a glaring light bulb.

Displays. As mentioned before, a display is a three-dimensional exhibit, such as an antique sewing machine with material and sewing notions artistically arranged. It can also take the form of a set that is built. For example, a wood pier with paper waves could be built for a nautical theme. A train station could be built for a transportation theme. A display can provide texture and depth. Many items will work as conversation pieces, promoting discussion among the guests. As with the wall decorations, displays will need to be spotlighted if the room is to be darkened.

Windows. Window decorations are not always necessary. Most simple luncheons require only decorations for the table and perhaps a few for the front. More elaborate affairs may desire to incorporate window treatments. Windows can be filled with greens (pruned from someone's holly bush), a candle, and a bow. They could have wreaths in them or be framed with twinkle lights. They can be garnished with tinsel garland, crepe paper, or big tissue flowers. Ornaments or sun catchers can be displayed. Crystal prisms could be used at a sunny morning brunch with interesting results.

Ceiling. Not every event will need treatment of the ceilings. Many simpler affairs will find it unnecessary and even distracting. For some events however, it is essential. An underwater theme needs extensive treatment of the ceiling to create the illusion of an underwater kingdom. Nets and fish and even perhaps a boat could be suspended from the ceiling, bringing the theme to life.

The most common treatment of the ceiling is with the use of crepe paper and balloons. This works nicely with birthday parties, showers, anniversaries, and themes that need lots of bright colors. Circus themes, fairs, Fourth of July luncheons, and Mexican fiestas all can be enhanced by crepe paper. Items like large tissue flowers, piñatas, color-coordinated balloons, and giant flags also can contribute to the bright festive appearance.

Inexpensive ribbon can be used in place of crepe paper if the event needs a classier presentation. It has the added advantage of not drooping and therefore can be put in place well beforehand. If carefully mounted and taken down, this can be reused at other affairs.

Stars made of card stock covered with gold or silver foil can be suspended from the ceiling. Snowflakes cut with six points, pressed, and lightly dusted with clear glitter can also look delightful dancing in the air. Thread used to suspend these items should be black or very dark. Clear plastic thread is not a good choice because it catches and reflects the light, making itself quite noticeable.

Another idea is to suspend objects from the ceiling. Giant, brightly wrapped gifts or upside-down umbrellas hanging in midair could be quite interesting. Another thought would be to rig a net that would at a given time drop confetti and ticker tape (interesting but quite a mess) or a mass of balloons to add excitement to the evening.

Lightweight items can be suspended from the ceiling by attaching a string or thread to a paper clip and inserting it between the panels and metal frame of a drop ceiling. Heavier items might need wire and a metal support or a screw eye in wood. Masking tape works well on lightweight items as long as it does not stay up for too long. The longer it stays up the more likely it is to mark. Scotch Tape is not a good choice for hanging things from the ceiling or wall because it tears easily, leaving pieces that rebel at removal.

Buffet tables. Buffet tables should be decorated in harmony with the banquet tables, in keeping with the theme and mood. Serving tables require better lighting than the banquet tables because people need to see well enough to choose their entrees.

Banquet tables. Consider the theme and mood in deciding which type of table arrangement would create the desired atmosphere. A warm and cozy evening homespun dinner, served family style by junior high girls dressed in colonial garb, calls for individual tables. On the other hand, a big bold and bright Fourth of July banquet might suggest long straight lines of tables.

Standard banquet tables can usually seat six to ten people depending on the size. If using standard banquet tables, keep in mind that they are not particularly wide, so make allowances for this when choosing the centerpiece. A pedestal arrangement, candles, and/or garlands work especially well.

Large round tables can usually seat ten to twelve people. Round tables can generally handle larger centerpieces because of the extra space in the middle of the table.

Card tables can be borrowed or rented. Card tables seat four and are useful when trying to create a cozy or romantic mood. Ice cream socials with red and white checked tablecloths can be enhanced by card tables because they capture the ice cream parlor look. Candelight spaghetti dinners with glass pop bottles thickly dripped with candle wax can also be embellished with the use of this type of table. Card tables work well with youth or adult functions, but they are not the best choice for a family event because many families have more than four members. Also their lack of stability becomes a factor with little children running about.

Banquet tables can be lowered on cinder blocks or other such support. This idea can be used to create a mid-eastern look. This idea can also be used to make a special table for children. For seating use pillows or rug squares or the floor.

Another idea is to use the floor or ground. Use blankets or towels on the ground to facilitate the mood of the event. Make sure to have chairs available for older folks and pregnant women who cannot sit on the floor. Have guests bring pillows if it is an event like a film night. Use this idea for beach ("Soak in the Sonshine") and picnic themes. This idea would need an active program with lots of audience interaction because sitting on the floor for long periods of time becomes very uncomfortable. Make sure drinks are served in mugs or other "hard to spill" containers.

Table Decorations

Tablecloths and place mats. Use goal, theme, mood, and color to decide the type of tablecloth that would be most appropriate. Place mats and runners can be used to add color to inexpensive white tablecloth rolls. Experiment with different shapes. Green construction paper could be fringed to form a grassy appearance for a nature theme. Giant flower petals can be cut from tissue paper forming an interesting place mat for the plate that would then take on the appearance of the center of a flower. Heavy manila paper cut into the shape of Texas would dramatize a Western theme.

Plates/cups. Paper plates are a good choice for a special event. The cleanup alone makes them worth their weight in gold. Plastic-coated plates are usually worth the extra cost especially if it is an occasion where people are dressed in nice clothes. Flimsy paper plates can give under the weight of food and can soak through. Many events, especially baby showers, wedding showers, and birthday parties, can use the picture or design from the plates for the motif. Simply repeat the motif in the center-pieces and the event looks quite "put together."

Do not overlook the use of solid colored plates as a decorating feature. They can deliver a great color impact as well as be versatile in producing creative illusions, as in the previous example of the center of the petal place mat. Green plates could give the illusion of a leaf on which a ladybug program is sitting. Black paper plates can be made to resemble musical notes.

China plates can also be used and can help reduce costs. They also can be useful if the food is likely to soak through a paper plate or if excessive cutting is required. The use of china will greatly increase the cleanup job so be sure that the kitchen crew is adequate. Check the location of the kitchen and make sure that the noise of washing dishes will not interfere with the program. Consult with the refreshment committee before firming up the decision to go with this option.

Flatware. There are many types of flatware. The most cost-effective choice is stainless steel flatware which many kitchens have on hand. Stainless steel flatware can also be borrowed, providing each piece is kept track of and promptly returned. One suggestion is to have each table hostess provide for her own table. That way all of the silverware belonging together stays together. Each hostess can then collect them when the dinner is through and take them home, dirty if necessary. Another thought is for each guest to be asked to provide their own flatware.

There also is the option to use plastic flatware. These add color and speed cleanup. Make sure the flatware will work with the menu chosen. Don't expect a plastic knife to cut through steak.

There are various ways of setting out the flatware. They may be wrapped in a napkin, or placed on the table, or colorfully displayed in a clear tumbler. They can be laid out in a pattern on the buffet table or placed in decorated baskets or bins.

Nut cups/favors. Nut cups and favors can be used to thread the theme into the decorations. Think of an object that can hold volume and which also coordinates with the theme. Hat boxes made of cut paper towel rolls would coordinate with a hat theme, for instance.

Favors can give an event a gracious feel. For example, give

netted potpourri tied with satin ribbon to ladies attending a bridal shower. Ideally favors should compliment the theme of the banquet or at least the atmosphere of the event. Favors can have a utilitarian use and also double as a take-home souvenir, like brightly colored chopsticks at a Chinese dinner. Favors can also be used as part of the centerpieces. These can be divided up after the event is over.

Place cards. Reservation place cards are little cards decorated thematically and set on a place to reserve it. These cards can be prelabeled and arranged on the banquet tables to facilitate assigned seating. They are also very useful if they are handed out to the guests with their name tags at the registration/name tag table. The guests can then position them on the places of their choice. This allows them to mingle with other guests without fear of losing their places. Without an alternative way of saving their seats, people resort to folding up chairs and leaning them against the table, which can rip the tablecloth. Or they will string coats and purses along the seats (usually leaving someone to "guard" the stuff). Reservation place cards can solve this problem easily and efficiently.

Lighting. Lighting is a major ingredient in setting atmosphere. Darkened overhead lights make the walls of the room fade away. Spotlighting of the displays makes people see what you want them to see. The options for lighting are extensive.

When making a decision on table lighting it is important to consider not only the theme of the event but also the atmosphere you are trying to create. Candles come in all sizes, colors, and shapes. Tall tapers generally lend an elegant look. Swirly tapers compliment a theme that is ornate. There are stately candles that resemble tall Greek columns and would make an interesting choice for a Roman or Ancient Civilization Banquet. Fat candles go well with a more casual, homey affair. Individual votive candles set at each place is another approach that is often overlooked. Green, red, and white votive candles can be picked up relatively inexpensively after Christmas.

Candles can be made to go with various themes. Sand candles can be made using a tray of sand. Wet the sand and use a drinking glass to punch a shape into the sand. Attach the wick and pour in hot wax. For variety add some shells. When the wax hardens dust off excess sand and use the candle for a sea/beach theme. Another example of a homemade thematic candle is the ice candle. Attach an inexpensive white taper or wick to an empty, clean, paper milk container. Pack this with cracked ice chunks and pour hot paraffin over it. After the wax hardens pour off the melted water and tear off the paper carton. The resulting candle has an interesting icy effect that would look excellent with a Winter Wonderland theme.

Sometimes candles can look rather stark on tables. Greens, cotton, tinsel, and other such material can soften the harsh line where the candles and table meet.

Table lighting need not always be limited to candles. This is especially true if the event involves children. Children tend to run and bump into things which could end up causing a real tragedy if fire were involved. Hurricane lamps, small table lamps, and strings of tiny white Christmas lights can be used with great success. Make sure that a table arrangement is chosen that would allow the cords to be grouped and taped to the floor so a safety hazard won't be created. Tiny white lights can border the buffet table or wrap around a garland running down the center of the table. Large Christmas lights can also be used especially if the colors are monochromatic. Kerosene camp lamps would look great at a Gold Rush Party. Crystal kerosene lamps with brightly colored oil could beautify a Christmas dinner. Flashlights can even be suspended from the ceiling to spotlight the centerpiece.

Lighting can also be incorporated in the centerpiece. This can be done simply by surrounding a fat red candle with holly and pinecones. It can also be done elaborately such as rigging a blinking light atop a cardboard lighthouse at an ocean banquet. Or constructing red/yellow/green stoplights for a transportation theme.

With the help of lighting you can transform a room into a whole new world. Candles on the table alone rarely provide enough light for mobility. This is especially a problem with a buffet where you have a multitude of people milling around with laden plates and hot coffee. Spotlighting displays and the stage area can help provide enough light so that people can move around without running into each other or tripping. Buffet tables should be more generously lit because people need to see the food well enough to make their choices. Do not, however, put the food on a buffet table in a separate room with the overhead lights on. The contrast is too great between the glaring light of the food room and the relative darkness of the banquet hall. People's eyes have trouble adjusting to light. Unless the mood is very bright and bold try to avoid overhead lights as they can be very harsh and dispel the atmosphere.

Centerpieces. The focal point of the table is the centerpiece. It is vital that it be correct in theme and color. Centerpieces can be whimsical, elegant, rustic, and so on depending on the mood of the event. They can be uniform or each different so long as a thread of continuity runs through. A luncheon using dolls as a theme can have different kinds of dolls on the tables as centerpieces. A collection of teddy bears may all be different, but each could have a color-coordinated ribbon around his neck or a prop such as a balloon.

Centerpieces can be put on double duty. For a Valentine party, ask several women to make heart cakes. Each cake will be different and thus provide conversation pieces yet have continuity because they are all hearts, and dessert has been provided to boot. Centerpieces can be used as door prizes to be given away to the winner of random drawings or quizzes. They can also consist of a container of favors, like a breadbasket filled with ornaments for the guests to take home.

The cost of the centerpiece can be defrayed in one of several ways. First it can be offered for sale at the event. This can be discreetly handled by making a simple announcement, in addition to a written note in the program. Another way of cutting costs is to borrow objects rather than buy them. Borrow teddy bears for a bear theme. Just make sure the owner's name is pinned on and that the owners know they are responsible for picking up their bears when the event is over.

Programs. Programs are important because they are a vehicle of communication. They build anticipation by giving people a glimpse of what is to come, especially if the program is cleverly written. They can include the way of salvation at an evangelistic event and perhaps a response card. They can give people an indication of when the breaks take place. I once attended a First Ladies' lunchon in Washington, D.C. Several of the ladies at my table stepped out at intermission but failed to return before Mrs. Reagan spoke. They did not know how long the break was. When they returned to the table and found Mrs. Reagan almost finished with her speech, they werre visibly angry.

Programs can also include a theme song or poem which is helpful if group participation is desired. This is a good place to give credit to the various workers who put on the event. It is also an appropriate place to give instructions or present opportunities. Information could be included concerning selling the centerpieces, or requesting help for cleanup. Programs provide mementos that are taken home and kept. If these programs are filed, they can be referred to in later years to glean ideas. I have revised and updated versions of banquets done thirty years ago by perusing my mom's and aunt's files.

Programs are an excellent vehicle to express creativity and underscore the theme. Programs can be made of card stock, construction paper, parchment, and a variety of other materials. They can be cut out to look like an object such as a star. They can be flat or three-dimensional. A hat program could be made by simply folding typing paper and setting it upright. A cocoon program could fold out into a butterfly. A paper bunny could be pulled from a flat paper top hat. Programs can be creatively attached. Materials like yarn, satin ribbon, gold cording, and staples could be used. A ladybug program could be attached with pipe cleaner antennae. A paper doll program could be joined together by tiny bows attached to her hair.

Cloth, lace, sandpaper, foil, ribbon, pom-poms — all add texture and make the programs interesting. Ribbon could be added to make the strings of an apron. Wiggle eyes could be pasted on snowmen and teddy bear programs. Sandpaper and tiny shells could be used in fashioning an ocean theme program.

Many times it is better to use cutting, pasting, or painting for the cover of the program, leaving any writing or words for the inside since it is easier to run off paper through a copier than card stock. Card stock generally requires a professional printer, which can increase the cost of an event quickly.

The lettering on the inside of the program can reflect the mood of the event as well. Country themes can use the dot lettering, and more glamorous affairs may require script calligraphy. Of course, simply typing the inside of a program is perfectly acceptable.

Offering envelopes. Offering envelopes can be used if an offering is the chosen method of covering costs. The envelope serves as a reminder for people to give. This is especially needed if the baskets are stationary at the back of the room. The object is not to apply pressure but to give people an obvious opportunity. Many times people have every intention of giving but just plain forget without something to bring it to mind. If possible, decorate the envelope thematically.

The place setting plan. After you have has decided which elements are going to be used, it is wise to sketch out the place setting plan. This aids in making placement decisions and helps communicate the arrangement to the helpers. Sometimes it will help to color in the sketch to make sure that the color balance is good. This will give confidence that the colors, textures, and other components are working together. Make sure that items placed on top of each other contrast so that they will stand out. For instance do not place a red heart program on a red plate. Either make the program pink or white, change the color of the plate, or set the red heart program next to the plate contrasting it with the white of the tablecloth.

Table arrangement. The next step is to figure out the arrangement of the tables. Make sure to keep in mind the goals and mood of the event because the way the tables are placed will have an effect on people's emotions. Of course there are other factors, such as the shape and size of the room and number of people attending that also have an effect on planning the placement of tables.

Tables can be arranged in long lines. This is more formal and allows for less interaction, but this arrangement can fit a lot of people in a small amount of space. The box shape is great for sharing and discussion. There are U-shaped arrangements, circular, diagonal, and so on. Generally it is a good idea to change the arrangement of tables for each event. This tends to separate the events in people's minds and thus keeps things interesting. Don't get trapped into thinking there is only one "right" way of doing things.

When planning the arrangement, make sure that visibility is not impaired. Do not put chairs behind posts or tables in cubbyholes. If these arrangements must be made to seat all of the guests, give time at the beginning of the program for chairs to be moved to an area of higher visibility.

The spacing between the tables is also important. If the tables are spaced too far apart, the interaction between the tables is wiped out, causing people to feel isolated. If tables are too close, people cannot maneuver easily, causing bumping, spilling, and a generally cramped feeling. If the hall is overcrowded by necessity, it is better to serve the meal using waitresses or at the very least have the tables dismissed one at a time. In a crowded situation where a buffet is used, a served dessert can relieve the bumping, scooting, and general congestion.

It is very helpful to sketch out a floor plan including table placements, stage, displays, buffet tables, chairs, and so on. The beauty of having the plan on paper is that people trying to help can do so more efficiently because all they need to do is glance at the plans and go to work. This avoids having a million questions attack the leader all at once.

Make sure to keep in mind traffic flow, so that people can easily get from one point to another, especially if there will be low lighting. Mark the location of various displays, making sure they are put where the eyes naturally fall. Safety considerations need to be checked also. Make sure that displays do not block emergency exits.

It is important to keep the plan flexible. Sometimes, ideas look great on paper but just do not work when actually set up. An arrangement might seem perfect in your head but might look too crowded or empty when actually set up in the room. Do not be afraid to change things around.

Setup. Ideally, the banquet hall should be set up the day before the event. That way if something just does not work, there will be time to remedy the situation. Then on the day of the event the workers will be relatively relaxed because they know that everything looks great. Getting the decorations set up the day before allows you time to get ready to go to this event and be calm enough to enjoy it. Finishing the decorations at 4:30 and then dashing home to change in order to be back at 5:30 will make you feel exhausted and might set you up as the next candidate for burnout. This extra leeway can also come in handy if someone has a brilliant last minute idea.

A possible exception to this rule involves crepe paper. Save crepe paper hanging until the morning of the event, especially in humid weather, because crepe paper is notorious for drooping.

The decorator should make sure everything that is needed has been brought to the setup session. Things like masking tape, scissors, string, and paper clips should be brought from home unless the church supplies have been previously checked. Make sure that you know where things are prior to the set-up time. Valuable time is wasted when a group of people show up at church to set up and no one knows where to find the supplies. It wouldn't hurt a bit if the coordinator arrived 10 minutes before everyone else. A frantic, ill-prepared leader does not inspire confidence. The idea is to be completely ready by the time the helpers arrive. That way their time will be used to the best advantage.

Keep the floor plan available so that the helpers can consult it and not the leader for directions in the placement of tables. If there are many tables to set up, the leader might want to set up one model table to serve as a guide.

WORKSHEET 13

Personnel Worksheet: Decorations

Event:	Theme:
Audience:	Event Title:
Date:	Goal:
Time:	Message:
Place:	Color:
Cost:	Mood:
Projected attendance:	Motif:
Dress:	Decoration budget:

Committees:	**Name**	**Phone**
Coordinator:		
Publicity:		
Registration:		
Refreshments:		
Agenda:		
Clean-up:		
Child care:		
Other:		
Decorations:		

Helpers:

Date of setup:
Time of setup:
Setup personnel:
Items to bring at setup:

WORKSHEET 14

Room Decorations

Outdoor entrance: Foyer:

Walls: Windows:

Ceiling: Floors:

Buffet table: Stage/front:

Arrangement of Hall: *(sketch layout of tables, displays, etc.)*

Projected attendance: ___
Number of tables needed: ___

WORKSHEET 15

Table Decorations

Tablecloth/place mats:

Flatware:

Cups:

Nut cups:

Programs:

Plates:

Napkins:

Place cards:

Favors:

Centerpieces:

Place Setting: *(Sketch an individual table including a place setting, center-piece, etc.)*

NINE

Refreshments

The role of food at a special event is more than just filling empty tummies. Eating and fellowshiping go hand in hand. Milling around a dessert table or chatting over a salad provide time for people to become acquainted and discover mutual interests. And visitors feel less conspicuous if they have a cup of coffee in hand. So don't overlook the value of food when planning your special event.

The purpose of the refreshment committee is to ensure that an appropriate menu is provided in sufficient quantities. Make sure the person recruited to handle this responsibility is very dependable. It is good to have several experienced people working on this, especially if it is a home-cooked meal. Much of their work cannot be done ahead of time which creates a potential high-anxiety situation. The group should also include some inexperienced help so that they can learn by observing these people in action. The experienced people need to be encouraged to train the new helpers so that talents are discovered and skills are developed.

If at all possible, the menu should reinforce the *theme*. Seafood entrees can be used with an ocean theme. Mexican dishes are a must for a Mexican fiesta. Gingerbread goes well with a pioneer theme. Keep in mind the *colors* of the event and reinforce them whenever possible. Use red punch for Fourth of July and yellow lemonade for a bright Daffodil luncheon. At no extra cost the food will reinforce the color impact of the decorations.

Of course you will want variety in the menu, and color can be sacrificed for a tasty dish. *Never* change the natural color of foods. Though green mashed potatoes might match the decor, they will appear contrived and unappetizing.

A special event becomes exciting when something unexpected happens. Consider refreshment surprises which might heighten the impact of the activity. For instance, sparklers in ice cream might be used to "snazz" up a dessert for the Fourth of July (make sure to check fire codes). For an ornate banquet you might want to try those fancy flaming desserts. Remember, refreshments are important not only to feed the body, but they can also add to the event as a whole.

Try to plan the menu so that some of the food can be made in advance. Make sure to test all new recipes. If freezing is desired, make sure to freeze some samples ahead of time to see if the quality of the food is affected.

It is a wise idea not to expect or ask the coordinator or the decorations chairman to prepare a main dish or any last-minute food. Their duties keep them busy right down to the wire, and they should not be expected to produce food too. Their contribution could be met by buying ingredients for the punch or providing a dish that could be whipped up well ahead of time.

The menu should be well thought out and the church kitchen should be double-checked to make sure that it is stocked with all the needed equipment and to see what should be brought from home. It would be smart to familiarize yourself with the kitchen so that you don't panic in the pressure of the event. Do not forget to make a note of what condiments will be needed and make provisions for providing them.

Methods of Acquiring Food

As previously mentioned in the registration section, there are three basic ways of acquiring food for a function: open potluck, assigned potluck and catered dinner.

Open potluck. "Open potluck" is where everyone brings whatever they want within certain general limitations. This is usually facilitated by a general announcement to bring a particular type of dish such as a salad or a dessert. The food committee fills in the extras, like punch or perhaps the meat.

Assigned potluck. The "assigned potluck" method places restrictions on the menu or on who is to bring what. People are assigned to bring a particular dish or a dish in a general category. This can be achieved by using a sign-up sheet where people sign up under the category they prefer. The sign-up sheet could include places to check off salads, side dishes, desserts, or main dish. Another method is to have people assigned according to the alphabetical order of their last names. A–E could bring main dishes, F–J could bring salads, and so forth. Food could also be assigned in a creative manner; try using foot sizes to designate which type of food is to be brought by whom! Another technique might depend on the refreshment committee calling at a later date to ask people what dishes they would like to bring.

Catered dinner. A catered affair is where the main audience brings nothing and the food is prepared by a small group of people, whether they be professionals or some good cooks at church. This method is preferable at wedding and baby showers, at receptions, and some formal banquets. Because all the food is bought beforehand and not donated as in the other options, this is the most expensive method, so consider your budget when making this choice.

A group of professionals can be hired to come and fix the meal on the premises. Or the group could meet at a restaurant and the establishment could provide the food. It is wise to send a scouting committee to various restaurants to taste the food and check on cleanliness, prices, and the facilities' compatability with the program. The commitee should come home with general floor plans from places that are serious contenders. These reports are then used in planning the program.

An event can also be committee-catered. This is where a committee is formed to handle the actual cooking. The men could be recruited to cook for a ladies' banquet. A group of women could put together food for a men's prayer breakfast. This method requires upfront funding, whether by ticket sales or special funds. If the event is to be catered by a group of people who do not do this professionally, it would be wise to plan a menu that can be prepared ahead of time. The more food prepared earlier, the less stress at the end and the greater the margin of safety.

Sometimes a wise way to organize this is to divide up the food, making different people responsible for different dishes.

One could be responsible for the desserts while another could take care of the salads. Each person would make enough for the entire group. These people can then work in their own kitchens and transport the food to the banquet hall.

Style of Service

The style of service is another important consideration. There are several options.

Buffet. A buffet is where all the food is set out on serving tables and people help themselves. This method is a must if the event is done in potluck style because the menu is not uniform. Be prepared to deal with a room crowded with tables or the semidarkness of a candlelight dinner. People need to be able to circulate easily. Consider excusing people one table at a time to get their food. That way everyone at a table gets up at once, and the buffet lines are not too long. Have the waitresses serve a uniform dessert. This allows people to remain seated for the remainder of the meal and not be bothered by people scooting past them.

If children are present at the function, encourage them to stay with their parents or an adult. Kids are notorious for having eyes bigger than their stomachs and have been known to overload their plates. Encouraging children to stay with their parents will cut down considerably on the spills and the accidents.

It is common courtesy to allow the speaker and his or her party to have the first place in line. It is not only an honor, but it also allows him or her plenty of time to finish before speaking.

Served. Food can be served using waiters and waitresses. The food is dished up in the kitchen and served. This is especially helpful if conditions are crowded. It allows guests to remain seated, avoiding congestion.

If the function is a potluck affair, the waiters and waitresses could also be responsible for collecting the food as the guests arrive. Servers can also double as greeters and act as ushers showing the guests where to sit.

The servers could be dressed to match the theme, bringing the event to life. A Thanksgiving Feast, for example, can have the servers dressed as pilgrims. At a circus dinner they could be dressed up as various performers. Little angels could grace a Christmas banquet. Simply wearing the colors of the event or matching outfits could add something special to the event.

Payment of these servers is optional as long as everyone's expectations are on the same level. It is nice to include a small thank-you present to those who helped, but this is not in any way mandatory. In most cases, just to be involved is reward enough.

Home style. This method consists of dishes of food being set on the table where guests pass them around and serve themselves. It works well in congested areas but it requires a uniform menu. It will not work with an open potluck.

Another way of implementing the home style of serving is to ask a number of people to commit to being table hosts. They would be responsible for getting the food from the kitchen and making sure that everyone had enough to eat. They might even be asked to bring the main dish. It is less confusing to have 12 people walking to and fro than 130. In addition, they would make sure that everyone at their table was introduced and made to feel at home. The secret beauty of this method is that the hosts have taken on the responsibility for not only the physical needs of their guests but the emotional needs as well.

WORKSHEET 16

Personnel Worksheet: Refreshments

Event: Theme:
Audience: Event title:
Date: Goal:
Time: Message:
Place: Color:
Cost: Mood:
Projected attendance: Motif:
Dress: Refreshment budget:

Committees	Name	Phone
Coordinator:		
Publicity:		
Registration:		
Decorations:		
Agenda:		
Child care:		
Clean-up:		
Other:		
Refreshments:		
Helpers:		
Servers:		

WORKSHEET 17

Refreshments

Menu: Drinks: Coffee
                                                   Juice
                                                   Soft drinks
                                                   Tea
                                                   Punch
                                                   Other

Method of acquiring food: *(circle one)*

    Open potluck   Professionally catered
    Assigned potluck   Committee catered

Style of serving food: *(circle one)*

    Buffet   Served   Hostess   Other:

Condiments needed: *(circle choices)*

    Cream   Butter   Catsup   Other:
    Sugar   Salt/Pepper Mustard

Layout of buffet table:

Equipment needed:

TEN

Agenda

The agenda committee is responsible for planning the event's activities — what happens and when. When will we eat? Who is the speaker? Is there special music? When do we sing? These are all questions that the agenda committee addresses. The agenda is extremely important because this is where the spiritual truth is communicated.

The Flow of Your Event
When planning an event, one needs to think in terms of flow. People are not ready emotionally, spiritually, or physically to receive the full impact of your event's message the minute they walk through the door. People come to an event in all sorts of moods. Some folks are angry, guarded, frustrated, nervous, or just plain distracted. Others are excited, open, and happy about the evening. Others just want to come and relax. So the challenge is to get this diverse group of people to stop thinking about all these extraneous things and focus on spiritual things. When a farmer plants a seed, he prepares the soil first so that the seed is planted in the most optimum conditions. So the goal of the agenda committee is to produce a program that helps people hear what is being said. This can be accomplished not only by what is being planned but also by the order of activities.

Humor is a wonderful mood equalizer. If something is funny and people respond to it by laughing, their moods are shifting and becoming equal. Humor puts people in a positive frame of mind. Light and interesting activities can be used to set the stage, reinforce the theme, and put people enough at ease to break down emotional barriers.

The mood of the event can now become a little more serious, reverent, or poignant. The people are now ready to listen—they are paying attention. This transition can be done with a special music number, a Scripture reading, or a poem. Sometimes an object lesson can quiet an event down even more. Thus by the time the speaker gets up, the mood has been set, hearts are ready, defensive walls are down, the soil is prepared.

The process is like a funnel: the mood should become more and more focused as time progresses. The basic principle of flow is this: light activities to heavy activities, fun activities to serious activities, with a gradual mood transition that is smooth, not abrupt.

Music, as stated before, is a great vehicle to create or change the mood. Music is to the ears what decorations are to the eyes. Music can be used to set a happy, cheerful atmosphere and then be used again to make a transition to a more serious tone.

Another key idea in developing the flow of an evening is to make sure to cut off the activities just after the interest level has peaked. Let the people enjoy the activity for awhile but change activities before there is any significant drop in interest. Leave them wanting more. Keep events moving but not rushed.

The Structure of Your Event

There are several ways to structure an event. A *centralized* event begins and ends with everyone doing the same thing at the same time. The activities follow a prescribed order. Most banquets and dinners are centralized affairs.

A *decentralized* event has many activities that are going on at the same time. People wander around and take part in whatever they wish. Picnics, fairs, carnivals, and some parties work best if done this way.

An event can combine these two structures by starting off with various decentralized activities and then bringing people together for a portion of the program. A decentralized opening has the added advantage of giving early arriving guests things to do right from the start. Then after running thirty to forty-five minutes worth of decentralized activities, the guests can be called together for a more formal program.

The Schedule of Your Event

Every event, no matter how simple, will benefit from the use of a schedule. Choose appropriate activities for the event, taking into account the goals that have been decided on. Place activities in an order which creates a smooth flow. Then check to see if the chosen activities will fit in the prescribed time frame. This is done by jotting down how long each activity is projected to take. Then subtract these times from the starting time and develop a list that gives approximate times for starting various activities. The importance of projecting the time cannot be overestimated. Without this, you have no way of knowing if the plan of events will take one hour or three. Remember too that a centralized affair, such as a banquet, should only last about two hours. If it is much longer, people will get antsy and your event will not be effective. A sample program might look like this:

Time	Activity	Personnel	Duration
7:00	Presession Activities	Luther/Larry	10 min.
7:10	Welcome	David	3 min.
7:13	Prayer	Phil	2 min.
7:15	Dinner		40 min.
7:55	Thank-you	David	5 min.
8:00	Song	Jan/Karen	5 min.
8:05	Door Prizes	Mike	10 min.
8:15	Skit	Senior High	10 min.
8:25	Song	Lori/Kathy	5 min.
8:30	Object lesson	Judy/Dawn	10 min.
8:40	Speaker	Dann	20 min.
9:00	Prayer/Dismiss	Pastor	

This schedule will become helpful during the event to see if things are progressing as they should be. The time estimates can be used to judge whether to quicken the pace or slow it down. If things are taking longer than anticipated, just shorten or delete an activity; however, do not allow the schedule to become so rigid that it hinders the work of the Holy Spirit. Its purpose is to provide information which would serve as a guide and aid in making decisions, not to be an impersonal dictator.

As people agree to take part in the program, place their names on the schedule beside the activity. Give a copy of this to the decorations committee, so they will know what to include in their programs. It is not necessary to give the decoration committee the minute-by-minute times, just the order of events (plus any titles of poems, skits, or messages) and the personnel. An event like a two-day seminar where there is free time obviously needs to have general times noted, as would most decentralized affairs. The guests, however, should not know the minute-to-minute times or it becomes hard to fudge with grace.

Other Responsibilities
Housing. The agenda committee should also be responsible for the housing of any guest speaker, performer, or missionary. If the group to be housed is very large, a subcommittee could be formed. People recruited to aid in housing should be given written information with exact details as to when and where the guests are to be picked up, what food is to be provided, the guests' schedules, and their names, if possible.

Personnel. There are several other positions that should be filled by the agenda committee. If music is to be a big part in the event, a *music coordinator* could be chosen to be in charge of the special music, background music, and any corporate singing. He could be responsible for finding appropriate music and drafting the personnel to perform it. He may enlist the help of a sound man who could aid in setting up the microphones and operating the sound equipment.

An *emcee* is necessary to introduce events and keep things moving on schedule. A friendly person with a good sense of humor who can think on his feet is ideal for this spot. This person needs to generate warmth. Sometimes the event coordinator takes on this responsibility. The advantage to this is that the coordinator already knows what is going on and does not need to be briefed. It would be better, however, if either the agenda committee head, or another well-informed person, could take this responsibility so the coordinator can be free to deal with unexpected problems.

A *photographer* may be recruited to record the event on film.

Consider getting slides rather than prints because they are cheaper to develop and can be shown to the congregation at a later date.

A *light man* may be needed if any special lighting is required. This person could also run film projectors and aid in the technical aspects of the program.

Since first impressions are so vital, especially with first-time guests, it is important to man the entrance of the event with a *greeter*. It is his job to make people feel warm and welcome. He can help seat guests if the seating is assigned. He can also pass out programs or favors. Make sure the greeter is briefed on the basic agenda of the event, plus other pertinent information such as, "Where do we put the baked beans?"

Greeters can be men or women or children, depending on the event. It is an added touch if the greeter is thematically dressed. Imagine pilgrims passing out programs at a Thanksgiving feast. Visualize a man in a safari suit greeting people with a monkey puppet at a jungle theme event. This can really bring the event to life.

Elements of Agenda

There are many things that can be included in a program. It is important to choose those activities that will accomplish the prescribed goals. Other factors to consider when deciding what to include are the size and age of the audience. The spiritual, emotional, and physical condition of the audience are also important factors. There are also cultural differences between congregations in various parts of the country. Sometimes, it is wise to submit the program to the pastor or leaders of the church, so they can make sure all the elements are appropriate.

Here is a list of various activities that could be included in the program. They are given in alphabetical order for easy reference.

Choral readings. A choral reading is a piece of poetry or prose, presented by a group of people, on occasion with choreographed motions. The oral chorus could deliver their piece from the front, or they can be spaced around the room or dispersed throughout the audience to deliver a stereo effect.

Concerts. Many colleges have traveling singing groups that can be booked to provide uplifting entertainment at a social.

Large churches might have enough musicians in their congregation to put together a concert. The church choir could perform a cantata or musical.

Contests. This activity is another opportunity to involve the guests as participants. For example: have a costume contest for a missions banquet or vote for a favorite poster. Pattern an evening after the Olympics and treat each table as a separate country. The "countries" would compete against each other sending various champions to participate in tests of skill or folly.

Craft activities. Craft activities can be used in many ways. They can take the form of a workshop to learn new skills or the sewing of a border on a farewell quilt at a good-bye luncheon. When employing this option in your event, make sure to have easy outs for people who do not feel comfortable participating.

Demonstrations. Demonstrations are usually instructional in nature. A craft or talent can be exhibited. A chalk artist can come in and draw. A potter can explain how a pot is made and apply it to the Christian life using Romans 9 as a text. A radio controlled airplane buff can demonstrate his airplanes at a Sunday School picnic. Demonstrations do not have to be spiritual in nature although it is great if some application can be made.

Discussion groups. Discussion groups are particularly useful in events like retreats where time is not a restraining factor. Each group needs a leader to keep conversation on track and to create or pose pertinent questions. This activity is especially effective when worked in conjunction with a speaker.

Door prizes. Door prizes can be bought, made, or donated. Many stores will donate items if their name is mentioned. Prizes can be awarded numerically or with humorous questions, matching stickers, random drawings, quizzing, or other arbitrary criteria.

Fashion show. These are particularly effective at women's events. They can be humorous or very classy. They can feature store wares or handmade articles. This idea can be adapted to a mission's banquet where costumes of the world could be displayed. They can also be limited in scope, as in using just hats or aprons, especially if the script is clever.

Films. Christian films can provide spiritual impact and can take the place of a speaker. Other types of films are light diversions for the purpose of entertainment. Make sure that there is nothing offensive in the movie. Make sure that a spare light bulb is brought and that the equipment for showing the film is in good working order. Usually bookstores have a list of films or Christian film companies where movies can be rented. Home movies of the pastor as a child or movies of church events can also provide delightful moments.

Food preparation. Cooking, baking, or preparing food can be used as an activity in an event like a slumber party. Popcorn balls or pizza can be made by the guests with great enjoyment. It can also be the focus of an event as in a taffy pull.

Free time. In events such as picnics or retreats, where there are various recreational activities going on at one time, it is appropriate to schedule a chunk of free time for people to get their bearings or take care of needs without the fear of missing something. It can be hard to gather people after free time, so regroup with an activity, such as singing. Or use a trumpet, bell, or anything that makes a loud noise. Posted or individual schedules help people know approximately how much time they have before the next event.

Games. Picnics and similar events are built around games. Games become optional at other events — such as a ladies' luncheon. A game or mixer at the beginning of the event can break the ice and get people talking to one another. Or games can be used to teach. Activities like matching missionary facts to the right missionary or piecing together a verse puzzle can help people learn painlessly.

Gift giving. A banquet is a special time to present the pastor or other leader with an appreciation gift or bonus. Thank-you gifts or flowers can be given to those who helped with the banquet. Gift giving can be incorporated in a game such as a white elephant gift exchange. Gifts can be given humorously to deacons, pastors, and other leaders of the church. The presentation should be done by someone especially gifted at being witty or clever. Gifts can be bought, donated, or made.

Guest involvement. There are many ways for guests to participate in the affair. They can be encouraged to wear assorted shoes at a foot banquet. They can vote in a mock election. They can be encouraged to come in costume. Or everyone could be asked to bring a kite and then spend the day flying them. The possibilities are endless.

Hikes. Hikes provide good activities for slumber parties, picnics, camp-outs, or retreats. They can be rugged walks through the brush, a stroll through a garden path, or nature walks with a guide explaining the wonders of God's great world. Hikes can stretch the imagination when combined with role playing. Children could be taken through high grass and role play the lion attack of David Livingstone, or creep to a well and gather a pitcher of water as King David's soldiers did centuries ago.

Hunts. There are many types of hunts, providing fun for all ages. Treasure hunts with clues scattered about could enhance a pirate or mystery theme. Candy hunts (make sure to use wrapped candy), and peanut hunts are an old-time favorite with kids. Scavenger hunts of all types lend themselves to some events.

People hunts offer a great variety of possibilities. Teachers can hide, with kids seeking, or everyone can hide with one person searching. All parents can hide with bags of candy, with kids hunting for the grown-ups all over the church, collecting candy as they go.

Music. Special music can be funny and light but is most valuable in changing the mood from light to more serious or reverent. Special music can be vocal, instrumental, solo, or in groups. It can be performed by children, adults, men, or women.

Group singing can be effective especially at events like a Christmas banquet where everyone knows the words. To allow for group participation, include words of songs that are not well known in programs or on an overhead projector.

Object lessons. Object lessons are short talks that take common objects and pull spiritual lessons from them. For instance, the process of sewing a dress could be compared to the Christian walk. An object lesson can be thematic in nature and add interest to the spiritual side of a program.

Panel discussion. To provide a panel discussion, you'll need a group of people knowledgeable about a certain subject. Compose a list of questions to pose before the group or have the audience ask questions to elicit a large range of thoughts on a certain subject. This is especially valuable when trying to apply a biblical principle to a practical situation. "How to Witness in the Workplace," "Dealing with the Empty Nest Syndrome," and "Hospitality" are all subjects suitable for a panel discussion.

Play/dramatic presentation. A play can be a children's production, an outside drama group, or a group of individuals. It can either be light entertainment or can be heavy with spiritual implications. Another approach to this activity is for a costumed person to take on the personality of another and tell his or her story in the first person. A man might dress up as a shepherd and tell the Christmas story from the shepherd's point of view. A "pilgrim" might tell of his ordeal during the first terrible winter. One by one a trio of men might rationalize why they just could not stop and help that poor man who had fallen among thieves. The possibilities are limited only by your imagination.

Poetry. Event themes can be built around poems. They can be spiritual in nature or thematic. Poems can be read singularly or in groups. They can be dramatically interpreted or delivered very simply.

Prayer. Prayer time at an event can provide opportunity to worship the Lord corporately. This can be particularly effective at an event such as a mission's conference where people's attention is focused on a particular area that needs to be brought before the throne of God. Prayer times can also develop a spiritual intimacy between a group of people and their Creator, especially if done in small groups.

The opening or closing prayer is a good opportunity to involve people who are too busy to become involved with anything that takes lengthy preparation. This is also a good opportunity for someone with little public speaking experience. I also always try to reserve one prayer for the pastor's wife, pastor, or leader. This gives the leader visibility for the benefit of any visitors and puts a stamp of approval on the event.

Puppet shows. Puppets are another medium that can be creatively used to communicate spiritual truth. Puppets work especially well with children but can be used with adults as well. Scripts can be written from scratch or adapted from the many children's musicals that are put out today. Puppet voices can be live or previously taped.

Readings. From Dr. Suess to Spurgeon, one may choose a funny or dramatic short piece to drive home a point or deliver a light moment. Readings can also reinforce the theme. Scripture readings are a good choice for the quieter, more serious side of an event. The Bible can be read as a narrative, or with two or more people providing voices, or corporately. Ideally it should be read or recited with great feeling and expression.

Rides. Rides are a great attraction (especially for kids) and can reinforce a theme or provide dynamite entertainment. There are hay rides, pony rides, camel rides, buggy rides, rides in fire engines or big trucks, boats, snowmobiles, and many others.

Role plays. Role plays are usually impromptu plays where people take on another character or personality and act out responses to various problems. These can be very helpful in events that are educational in nature such as workshops or retreats. These are best done when people know each other well enough not to be too self-conscious.

Sharing/praise times. This activity works well with a smaller group. People are asked to respond to a question usually spiritual in nature. This activity works best when moods have been neutralized and emotions warmed up. Otherwise, people may feel that they are being put on the spot.

Skits. Skits are short, usually funny plays designed for light entertainment. A humorous skit aids the spiritual impact of the evening by putting people into a relaxed frame of mind where they are more willing to hear the message.

Slide show. The slide show is most commonly used by missionaries but can also be used in a variety of ways. Pictures of Vacation Bible School can be taken and shown at the closing program. The story of the Nativity can be shot on slides and then presented with music and narration at a Sunday School Christmas program. Slides can also be used to remember past church times at an anniversary dinner.

Speaker. Most banquets rely on a speaker to present a devotional or talk. Typically the speaker gives his presentation toward the end of the program, after hearts have been softened. This is usually the spiritual input of the evening. If at all possible encourage the speaker to incorporate a message that corresponds with the theme. At the same time do not limit him to it, just in case God has laid something else on his heart.

Personal testimonies can also be used as the spiritual input of the evening. A testimony is a personal account of what God has done in someone's life. This can include someone's conversion experience or something significant the Lord taught him or her through an experience.

Speakers can be people in the congregation, pastors from other churches, missionaries, etc. They might come from a nearby Christian college or seminary. Find out whether the speaker has a set fee or expects an honorarium. This is an area where good, upfront communication is essential. Without it, you will be in for a sticky situation. Some prefer a free will offering; others will accept whatever you offer them. Others will accept nothing at all. If a speaker is coming from any distance, you should insist on paying his expenses. Usually it is not necessary to pay people who attend the church, unless, of course, they are famous or do this for a livelihood. Then it is appropriate to offer them money. Another possibility is to give an appreciation gift to the speaker. This can be a dinner for two certificate, a book, a bouquet of flowers, or whatever you can think of that will communicate heartfelt thanks.

Beforehand, tell the speaker the approximate time allotted for his message. A devotional is usually ten to fifteen minutes in length. A talk, speech, or sermon can go from twenty to forty-five minutes and be much more involved. If you are planning on fifteen minutes and your speaker is planning on forty-five, and you don't communicate, he will be merrily speaking on while you are pacing the floor like a caged lion. I've done this—I know. Also give your speaker a clue as to appropriate attire for the event. Otherwise, he will have to guess.

If the speaker is coming from out of town, it is the agenda committee's duty to provide housing and meet any transportation needs. Make sure to communicate with the speaker so that he knows who will meet him, where he will be staying and generally what to expect.

Sports. Volleyball, softball, and horseshoes are a must for a Sunday School picnic. Events like basketball and softball marathons can use sports as the main attraction to draw folks in to hear a Gospel presentation. Events like retreats and slumber parties can also benefit from a hardy athletic contest. There are many different types of sports to choose from: swim meets, croquet, basketball, volleyball, horseshoes, shuffleboard, golf, football, softball, tennis, badminton, Ping-Pong, skating, skiing, sledding, darts, bowling, and hockey (to name a few).

Talent shows. Talent shows can really involve the congregation. They can be humorous or serious in nature. Have people sign up and then spend an evening exploring everyone's hidden talents. It is appropriate to find out enough about the participant's material to be sure that there are no duplicates and that the selections are suitable.

Thanks and appreciation. Sometime during the event a few moments should be dedicated to recognizing and thanking those responsible for producing the event. It is the agenda committee's job to thank the coordinator for a job well done. Flowers, plants, or other tokens can be given if desired. The coordinator may wish to thank the many helpers and her committee heads.

Videos. Videos can be funny or serious depending on your needs. Professional videos could be rented and used at slumber parties and similar events. You can also make your own videos, recording events or producing a story. Videos are tied to the small screen and thus are not conducive to large audiences.

Work projects. This is an activity rarely paired with special events these days. In pioneer days, however, house raisings were not only a time when all pitched in to aid a friend but were also great social gatherings. A familiar application of work projects are sewing and mending bees. A task, such as raking up the leaves on the church grounds, can be transformed into a party if a contest is held to see which Sunday School class can create the biggest pile. Prizes could be awarded, perhaps a gilded rake. Add a buffet table and, presto, the work gets done and everyone has a good time.

Writing activities. It is sometimes appropriate to include activities that involve writing. Guests could be given the opportunity to sign cards to send to missionaries. Thank-you notes could be written to the pastor. A Valentine party might provide time to write notes of appreciation to each other. This idea can be facilitated by having various tables set up with equipment and manned with people to encourage and instruct people. Make sure to dedicate enough time for people to complete the project. This activity works best in a decentralized affair.

WORKSHEET 18

Personnel Worksheet: Agenda

Event: Theme:
Audience: Event title:
Date: Goal:
Time: Message:
Place: Color:
Cost: Mood:
Projected attendance: Motif:
Dress: Agenda budget:

Committees:	Name	Phone
Coordinator:		
Publicity:		
Registration:		
Decorations:		
Refreshments:		
Child care:		
Clean-up:		
Other:		
Agenda:		
Music coordinator:		
Emcee:		
Sound man:		
Light man:		
Photographer:		
Greeter:		
Special speaker/group:		
Housing:		
Other:		

WORKSHEET 19

Agenda

Activities:

Music:
    Background music:
    Special numbers:

Schedule:

Time	Activity	Personnel	Duration

ELEVEN

Child Care, Clean-up, and Finances

No matter how well you have planned your program or special event, you could face disaster if you overlook the details mentioned in this chapter. Well prepared committees for child care, cleanup, and finances can head off problems before they occur.

Child Care
Providing adequate child care is integral to many special events.

Who will watch the kids? Workers can be found by asking for volunteers. Women outside of church can sometimes be hired. Arrangements with other churches could be made to trade a baby-sitting team. "We will provide sitters for your missions conference if you will provide sitters for ours." This system allows all members to attend the meetings at their own churches. Teenagers are another group that can be tapped — either individually recruited or approached as a group. If teenagers are used, at least one adult should be in the vicinity in case an emergency arises.

The child care committee should plan the details of how the care should be organized, recruite personnel, and make all necessary preparations. It is important for the child care workers to arrive at least 15 minutes before the event is to start. They need to be well briefed to project a competent air. Make sure to label bags *and* children! Masking tape works well in this capacity. Names can be taped to the backs of children so the labels aren't easily removed. It is also wise to have crackers or a snack on hand to beat hunger and create an activity that will break up the time. It is important to have extra diapers and wipes. It is also wise to have plastic bags handy to bag damp clothing.

The child care committee might want to employ the use of a nursery sign-up sheet. This would include such pertinent information as the child's name, parent's name, whether the child is nursing or bottle-fed, a description of the diaper bag, and space for miscellaneous instructions.

Child care can go beyond simple baby-sitting and become a children's ministry during the event. Games, crafts, stories, puppet shows, films, and so on can be included.

Cleanup

The least glamorous committee of any event is, without a doubt, the cleanup crew. The Lord Himself gave us an example of humble service rendered in love by washing the feet of His disciples. He demonstrated that this lowly service is no less honored in His eyes than the most widely acclaimed or highly visible ministry.

The cleanup committee, consisting of those not involved in the other committees, can give a real lift to the morale of others and help alleviate burnout. The decorations committee may have spent the better part of the previous twenty-four hours at the hall. They should not be expected to do the cleanup too. Likewise, those preparing the food should not have to wash the dishes as well.

The cleanup committee chairman should enlist help to take down the decorations, sweep or vacuum the floors, return the room to its normal arrangement, and clean up the kitchen.

The chairman of the decoration committee should be consulted before the event to determine what is to be done with the decorations. Some may need to be returned to those who have loaned them. Some may need to be stored for future use, and of course, some will need to be tossed out.

Guests, particularly the men, can be asked to take down the chairs, or to rearrange them. Or the chairman may want to make arrangements ahead of time by asking specific individuals to do each job.

A fresh, cheerful kitchen crew coming in after the event to give a helping hand can be a real boost to the food committee.

Every dish should be clean and put in its proper place and the floor mopped. Proper cleanup after the event is a must in keeping a good relationship with the deacons, the janitor, etc. It is the final touch to a successful, happy event.

Finances

Keeping an accurate financial record of a special event is critical. You need to know what your event has cost. This will enable people to be reimbursed promptly. It is also helpful when planning the next function because people can get an idea of how extensive an event can be for the amount of money budgeted. Ideally it is a good idea to have all items listed on one piece of paper rather than trying to keep a clear picture of the money situation using a million and one scraps of paper. A manila envelope with a clasp can aid in centralizing the receipts.

Many times the coordinator of an event may wish to keep track of the finances personally, especially if the event is simple. If the event is more involved, it may be better to enlist the aid of a treasurer to keep track of these details. This duty could fall on the assistant-coordinator or be taken care of under the umbrella of the registration committee. In any case this job needs to be handled efficiently so that no one will have occasion to think or speak evil.

Options in Covering Expenses

There are several options to consider in deciding how to cover the expenses of a given event. Each has advantages and disadvantages. The leadership must make sure to choose the one that will best accomplish the goals of the event.

Offering. An offering can be taken either by passing a basket or by providing offering envelopes to be placed in stationary baskets. This method makes it possible for people on tighter budgets to attend the function. It also allows people to place in the offering whatever amount the Lord lays on their hearts. This frees people up to invite as many guests as possible because they do not have to pay a set price per guest. However, this method requires front money to be obtained from somewhere. The event must be backed by a group or individual who is willing to pay any bills that are not covered by the offering. This method can be exciting if done in faith. It is interesting to see the Lord provide and meet the need. It also has the advantage of appearing less commercial than tickets or admission. Make sure to mention in the publicity that an offering will be taken. People will then come mentally and physically prepared to give. Do not say that an event is free and then hard sell an offering. Guests will feel that they have been conned.

Sponsor. The church, an individual, or a group could decide to donate the money to finance a function. This is a great method for an evangelistic event where you do not want the public to think that you are interested in them for their pocketbooks.

Tickets and admission. Another method commonly used is the sale of tickets or the charging of admission. These methods are especially helpful when an event is being catered and front money is required in large quantities. The difference between tickets and admission is that admission is collected at the door whereas tickets are sold beforehand. This event will limit the number of visitors that will be invited. Make sure the method of financing an event is consistent with the chosen goals. If at all possible, try to provide a scholarship for people who may not be able to afford to come. Be very careful not to make these people feel like charity cases. Remember that it is difficult to admit financial need. This is best done quietly.

Combination. An event can be presented on an either/or basis. People could be asked to bring either a dish or a certain amount of money. Then those that have the time can make food while those who find fixing a dish inconvenient can fulfill their obligation by giving cash. This works well if there are a lot of working women or single men in your group.

You might also ask the guests to bring a dish *and* some dollar amount. In such a case the money could provide the drinks and/or main dish and other extraneous items. The guests could fill in the side dishes and dessert.

Spinning Straw into Gold

The folk tale of Rumplestiltskin is a well known story in which a young miller's daughter was asked to spin straw into gold. Many times people are faced with the same perplexing problem of putting on an event with a very tight budget. There are several ways to stretch the Lord's dollar to its most fruitful use.

Creativity can replace money. If an event has a shoestring budget, choose themes that lend themselves to inexpensive materials. A country theme might require yarn ties on the programs rather than satin ribbon. Depend on clever ideas that can be cheap or free. For example, a fall harvest party is needed for a children's group. To say that there is a limited budget is an understatement. Try spreading a bag of hay, donated by a farmer, on the floor and serving table. A basket of apples on its side, which could be bought and later eaten by the decorator, could be placed in the middle of the buffet table and voila you have a centerpiece. Bright orange paper napkins could be placed in church owned baskets. Corn stalks, also donated by a farmer, could be placed around artistically. The food could be brought by the children. The room could be completely transformed (although it would be a nightmare to clean up) all for a cost of less than ten dollars. (Caution: This idea can be hard on a group that has allergy prone people.) Pouring money on an event does not necessarily make it better although it does give a wider range of choices.

Borrowing. Not everything used in an event needs to be bought. Borrowing items can be a helpful alternative. Centerpieces, card tables, pictures, lights, etc. can all be borrowed as long as tremendous care is taken in making sure things are not damaged or lost. Do not borrow things that are so expensive they cannot be replaced. Do not use things that are sentimental to the owner, unless the owner is willing to take the risk. Make sure that items are labeled and returned promptly.

Double duty. Another way of cutting costs is to have items serve several purposes. A cake could be used as a centerpiece as well as a dessert. A centerpiece could serve as a door prize. Slightly used candles can be stored for later events. The more times an item is used, the cheaper each individual use becomes. Use decorations and extra food for other ministries. Extra mileage can be obtained by recycling decorations for the Sunday School bulletin boards. Flowers could be used for hospital calls, and extra cookies could be used on visitation, or consumed by the children's ministries.

The Stone Soup Principle. There is a classic tale of three soldiers who upon arriving in a village were told that there was no food to be had. The soldiers declared, "No matter, we can make soup from stones." The villagers were very intrigued by this as they watched the men place three round stones into a boiling pot of water. The villagers gradually contributed vegetables that they had been hoarding to make the soup "even better."

This story illustrates the principle that people can become very willing and generous to aid financially in an event once they become involved and catch the vision of an event's potential. This only works effectively when people have adopted the event as "theirs." It is a phenomenon that must come from the heart because coerced financial support backfires, leaving people feeling trapped and used.

WORKSHEET 20

Child Care

Event:
Date:
Time:
Place:

Method of Payment: (*circle one*)
Donation   Fee ____   Volunteer   Sponsor

Cost:
Projected: Actual:

Attendance:
Children expected: Children attended:

#Kids	Age	Personnel/Phone	Snacks	Activities
	Nursery			
	Toddlers			
	2/3 Year			
	4/5 Year			
	Primary			
	Junior			

WORKSHEET 21

Cleanup

Event:
Date:
Time:
Place:
Committee budget:

Committees:	**Name**	**Phone**

Coordinator:
Registration:
Decorations:
Refreshments:
Agenda:
Child care:
Other:

Jobs:	**Personnel:**

Kitchen cleaned:
Tables and chairs:
Floor vacuumed/swept:
Restore furniture to previous position:
Other:

WORKSHEET 22

Finances

Event: **Date:**

Methods of acquiring funds: *(circle choice)*

Offering   Sponsor   Tickets   Admission

Front Money Record

Name	Amount	Received	Returned

Committee Expenditure Record

Department	Budget	Cost
Publicity		
Registration		
Decorations		
Refreshments		
Agenda		
Miscellaneous		
TOTAL		

WORKSHEET 23

Committee Expenditure Report

Event: Department:
Date: Chairman:
Budget: Total Expenditure:

Itemized List of Expenditures

Item	Cost

SECTION TWO:
Ideas

This section contains the extensive, detailed plans for eight common events. In most cases there are several ideas from which to choose. Select and adapt those ideas that will work with your set of needs.

Christmas Banquet

Event:	*Christmas Banquet*
Theme:	*Gifts*
Title:	*God's Gift Christmas Banquet*
Audience:	*Adults or general*
Goal:	*Celebration, fellowship, evangelism*
Color:	*Red and gold (with touches of white and green)*
Mood:	*Heavy, elegant, glitzy*
Motif:	*Presents, bows, wrapping paper*
Message:	*God's greatest gift to mankind, and to each of us, was sending His Son to provide us with eternal life.*

Publicity

Announcement ideas: Give the pastor a present to open. Inside is a framed announcement. He can read this to the congregation to announce the event.

Displays: Stick lightweight, empty, wrapped boxes all over walls with tags that tell bits of information.

Flyers/Invitations: Print information on one side of paper and paste wrapping paper on the other side. Fold it in thirds so that the wrapped side completely covers the inside information, resembling a wrapped present.

Bulletin Board/Poster: Use white, red, and gold printed wrapping paper for the background of a bulletin board. Attach a gold garland to the border. Tack a red foil-wrapped package (3-D) in the middle. Write the information on the tag.

Registration

Table Decorations: Red and gold boxes wrapped and arranged attractively on a red tablecloth.

111

Sign-Up Sheet:

1. Paste heavy white paper to gold foil-covered 11 x 14 inch poster board in such a manner as to create a gold border. Add gold fabric trim if you want to really get fancy. Use red lettering.
2. Use white card stock with red crinkle ribbon to create columns.

Name Tags: Make to resemble tiny gifts. Use white card stock and red and gold crinkle ribbon.

Refreshments

Menu: Ham
            Sweet potatoes
            Green Jell-O salad
            Green beans
            Homemade rolls
            Cake (Cakes can be decorated to look like gifts)

Drinks: *Coffee*
           Red Punch

Style of service: Waitresses dressed in red dresses, white aprons, and gold jewelry. Serve the main meal on a buffet table, but let the waitresses serve dessert, coffee, and drinks.

Decorations

Outdoor Entrance: Place luminaries along the walk and steps. Decorate rails with gold garland. Place a wreath on the door. Garnish the wreath with red bows, tiny gold or red packages, and white twinkle lights.

Walls: Green wreaths and red bows, garnished with little packages wrapped in red foil.

Windows: Large red candles and greens

Ceiling:

1. Suspend gold garlands and foil-wrapped gifts.
2. Hang gold foil stars.

Displays:
1. Gifts (use red and/or gold, plain and/or print wrapping paper)
2. Christmas trees (use only red and gold decorations)
3. Create a display of gold, frankincense, and myrrh in decorative brass containers.

Stage/Front: Center a podium between two Christmas trees. Decorate the trees with red and gold balls, gold garland, red bows, white twinkle lights, and a gold star on top. Arrange red and gold wrapped presents underneath the tree. Position a bouquet of pine and holly fronds in front of the podium with a large red bow.

Banquet Tables: Arrange in long rows.
- *Tablecloths:*
  1. Red paper tablecloths with gold place mats (use gold doilies or make from gold foil wrapping paper)
  2. White paper tablecloths
- *Plates:* Red
- *Napkins:* Red
- *Flatware:* Wrap in napkin and tie with gold cord
- *Cups:* Clear tumblers
- *Nut Cups:* Tie up candy in a square of gold wrapping paper and crinkle ribbon.
- *Place Cards:* White cards with red bows
- *Centerpieces:*
  1. Form garland of pine boughs and holly, tuck in little raisin boxes wrapped in gold foil with gold ribbon. Group assorted brass candlesticks with red tapers. (Use fat red candles if you cannot obtain enough brass candlesticks.)
  2. Group three to five presents (wrapped in assorted red/gold foil paper) in the center of the table on a bed of greens. Put a red votive candle at each place setting. (This treatment works especially well with a round table.)
  3. Dip fruit, leaves, pinecones, seed pods, etc. in thick gold paint. Drain and allow to dry. Attach gilded objects to gold painted base with hot glue gun and picks. Place this arrangement on a bed of greens and garnish with red velvet bows.
- *Programs:* Cover index cards (5" x 8") with gold foil and glue on red ribbon and bow. Insert information pages that have been written in a fancy calligraphy script. Attach with staple.

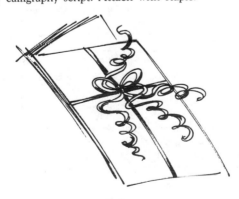

Agenda

Schedule: 7:00–9:00 P.M.

Time	Activity	Duration
7:00	Guess What's in the Gift?	10 min.
7:10	Carols (two)	5 min.
7:15	Welcome	5 min.
7:20	Pass the Gift	10 min.
7:30	Prayer	5 min.
7:35	Dinner/Gift Exchange	40 min.
8:15	Humorous Gifts	10 min.
8:25	Special number	5 min.
8:30	Scripture reading	5 min.
8:35	Devotional	25 min.

Music:

Background Music: Christmas carols (especially instrumental)

Special Music:

1. Carols (print lyrics in program)
2. "The Gift Goes On" by Claire Cloninger and Ron Harris (published by Ron Harris Music)
3. "We Three Kings" (traditional carol)
4. "Gift Wrapped" by Barbara Pence (published by Cair Paravel Music)

Activity Ideas:

- *Greeter.* Have the greeter, dressed in red, hand out little homemade Christmas ornaments.
- *Guess What's in the Gift.* Prepare a table with various numbered gifts. Allow guests to shake and/or rattle to try to figure out what is in the packages. Have them record guesses on paper. Announce the winner (the one with the most correct answers) after dinner.
- *Pass the Gift.* Prepare several gifts in several layers of boxes and wrappings. Have the group of guests stand in a circle. Have them pass the presents around while music is being played. When music stops, guests holding presents have ten seconds to start to unwrap the present. Then the music starts and they must pass on the present. This continues until the guests finally open the gifts. These gifts are prizes to be kept.
- *Humorous Gifts.* Have a person with a good sense of humor compile a group of amusing gifts for various well-known people in the congregation (such as the pastor, staff, and deacons).
- *Scripture Reading.* Choose a Nativity passage. This can be done by one individual or by a choral reading group.
- *Gift Exchange.* Number each name tag. Have each guest bring a gift. Collect them at the door. Randomly number each gift. Just before dinner pass out the wrapped gifts. (Make sure to give guests a gift that does *not* match their number). Each person must try to find the owner of the present he is holding and locate the gift that matches his number. He may then open the gift that matches his name tag and keep the gift.

International Missions' Banquet

Event:	*Missions' Banquet*
Theme:	*International children*
Title:	*Jesus Loves the Little Children of the World*
Audience:	*All ages*
Goal:	*Stir up interest in missions. Acquaint the people with the missionaries and update them on what is going on in their fields.*
Color:	*Bright colors: red, blue, green, yellow*
Mood:	*Splashy, bright*
Motif:	*Flags, international costumes, children*
Message:	*Jesus loves the children of the world. What can we do to tell them about Him?*

Publicity

Announcement Ideas: Set up a different international doll on the side of the podium every week. Have the pastor mention that this is to remind us of the upcoming mission banquet.

Bulletin Board/Poster Ideas:

1. Run a poster contest in the Sunday School. Display posters throughout the church. The night of the banquet let all guests vote (secret ballot) for a winner in each division (preschool/kindergarten/primary/junior). Award ribbons to the winners.
2. Pepper the area with construction paper flags containing bits of information.
3. Garnish bulletin boards with international dolls.

Registration

Table Decorations: White tablecloth with flags and dolls from other lands.

Name Tags: Little flags

Sign-up Sheet/Poster: Have people sign up on construction paper flags. Each flag can represent some type of dish to bring (main dish, side dish, salad, dessert, or other.)

Refreshments

Menu:	Potluck of international foods. (Label each food with its name and country on a paper flag.)
	Rolls
	Green salad

Drinks: Coffee
 Tea
 Punch (red)
Style of Service: Buffet
Condiments needed: Cream, butter, sugar, salt, pepper
Servers: Waiters and waitresses should be dressed in international outfits. They should keep the buffet table full and tidy. They can also be responsible for clearing off banquet tables and serving beverages.

Decorations

Outdoor Entrance: Line entrance with international flags.
Walls: Decorate with flags, travel posters, and displays of handmade posters grouped together in age categories so that guests can vote. Walls can also be decorated with child cutouts. These are made (perhaps during Sunday School) by laying children down on paper and tracing them. They are then colored to resemble those children. These can be cut out and taped (with masking tape) to the walls.
Windows: Little flags or international dolls.
Ceiling: Hang flags or banners.
Stage/Front: Decorate with flags, streamers, and a large multicolored bow at the podium. Cut large six-inch letters spelling out the title of the event or mission theme. Tape this to the wall at front of room.
Buffet Table: White tablecloth with international flags.
Banquet Table:

- *Tablecloth/Place mats:* White tablecloth with construction paper place mats made up to look like a variety of international flags.
- *Plates:* Use standard white plates. If programs are being handed out, set plates on the buffet table. If programs are being placed on tables, insert white plates between them and place mats to provide contrast.
- *Flatware/Napkins:* Multicolored napkins (red, green, yellow, blue) can be perched on forks.
- *Place Cards:* Write names on slips of yellow or white paper. Attach to toothpicks and stick into large colored gumdrops

- *Cups:* Clear tumblers (not set out on tables but served).
- *Nut Cups:* Use commercially made nut cups of various colors (blue, green, red, yellow). Fill with peanuts, M&M's and Skittles (for color).
- *Programs:*
  1. Paste scraps of material or construction paper to card stock to create flags. They can be uniform or varied.
  2. Cut out card stock in a shape that resembles various children of the world: Indian child, Chinese child, African boy, Dutch girl. Either

watercolor children or use construction paper, yarn, and fabric to add texture to program covers. Inside pages should be cut to fit the shapes of the program covers.

- *Centerpieces:*
  1. Buy or borrow little international dolls. Set singly on table or in groups of three. Place on a bed of multicolored crinkle ribbon.
  2. Little international flags placed on a wide red ribbon runner that goes the length of the table.
  3. Combine the two ideas above.

Agenda

Schedule: 6:00–8:00 P.M.

Time	Activity	Duration
6:00	Presession activities	20 min.
	Missionary Match	
	Flag Match	
	Missionary Notes	
	Poster Vote	
6:20	Welcome/prayer	5 min.
6:25	Dinner	40 min.
7:05	Special music	5 min.
7:10	Thank-you's, Poster awards	5 min.
7:15	Door prizes	10 min.
7:25	Children's oral presentation	10 min.
7:35	Special music	5 min.
7:40	Panel discussion or speaker	20 min.
8:00	Pray and close	

Music:
- *Background Music:* Play international music, maybe the anthems from countries around the world.
- *Special Music Suggestions:*
  1. "People Need the Lord" by Greg Nelson and Phill McHugh (published by River Oaks Music)
  2. "Here Am I Send Me" by John Purfoy (published by Word)

Presession Activities: When guests arrive, have the room set up with various booths or tables, each manned with someone who can encourage people to become involved and explain the activity. Suggestions follow:
- *Flag Match Game:* As guests arrive, give them a list of twenty-five countries. On a table in back of the room have pictures of flags or actual miniature flags numbered and on display. Have guests try to figure out which flag goes to which country.
- *Poster Vote:* Set up a small table where ballots can be cast for the displays of posters the children have created. Announce the winner after dinner.
- *Missionary Notes:* Set up chairs and a table (supplied with pens and paper) to encourage guests to write notes to the missionaries. Have on display recent letters from missionaries.

- *Missionary Match:* (Game for one person at a time.) Write the names of four to six missionaries on separate pieces of construction paper. Prepare a stack of 3" x 5" cards with various facts (one fact per card) about the missionaries. These facts can include pictures of them, the names of the countries in which they serve, the type of ministry that they perform, etc. The object of this activity is to match the facts with the right people by placing the fact card on the correct missionary sheet. Prizes (little pieces of candy from a grab bag) can be awarded for perfect scores.
- *Touring the Displays:* If a missionary or group of missionaries are invited to this affair, they will usually have booths or displays of their own to set up. This presession time is a great time to view their exhibits.

Other Activities:
- *Greeter:* The greeter should wear an international outfit.
- *Kids in Costume:* Have all children wear international dress. Prizes could be awarded for best costume, if desired.
- *Door Prizes:* Using information gleaned from missionary displays, compile a list of questions about the missionaries. Read questions to the audience. Guest with the first correct answer wins a door prize.
- *Panel Discussion:* If several missionaries are at your church, try a panel discussion. Have an emcee ask questions of the missionaries and then open it up to questions from the audience. Conclude with pastor giving a few words challenging people to pray for and support the missionaries.
- *Children's Oral Presentation:* Have a choir of children, each dressed in a different international costume. Focus on three to five missionaries. These could be ones at your conference or ones out on the field that your church supports. If using missionaries that are attending the banquet, have them get involved with this presentation.

Here is the basic formula for this oral presentation:

All:	Sing "Jesus Loves the Little Children of the World"
Child 1:	(Dressed in outfit from country he is representing) I am *(native name).* I live in the country of *(name of country).* There are over *(population of country)* people in our land. We live *(give description of housing).* We *(give another interesting fact about country).* We *(give basic spiritual plight of land, such as, "We worship trees and rocks. I am afraid of the evil spirits that rule the night.")* Who will come and tell me about Jesus? Someone said that He loves me.
All Children:	Whom shall I send and who will go for us?
Child 2:	Here I am, send me! I am *(name of missionary).* The
(or missionary)	Lord called me to be a missionary when I was *(age)* years old. *(Give one or two more pertinent facts about the missionary.)* I so want to tell the children of *(name country)* that Jesus loves them.

Repeat for two to four more missionaries. End with all children singing, "Jesus Loves the Little Children of the World."

Mother-Daughter Banquet/Ladies' Luncheon

Event:	*Mother/Daughter Banquet or Ladies' Luncheon*
Theme:	*Hats*
Title:	*Bonnets and Bows Banquet*
	Hats Off to Mom!
Audience:	*Women and girls*
Goal:	*Fellowship, challenge, recreation, and perhaps evangelism*
Color:	*Wheat and cranberry*
Motif:	*Hats*
Message:	*Just as hats serve our purposes, we have the privilege of serving the purpose of our Master.*

Publicity

Announcement Ideas: Have a woman come up from a side door each Sunday wearing a different hat—the more outlandish, the better. Have her make the announcement.

Displays: Hang real hats on walls. Pin information on them.

Invitations:

1. Print information on paper and fold up like paper hat.
2. Print (fancy script) information on tan paper and glue to cranberry paper in such a manner that the cranberry paper forms a border. Watercolor any sketches of hats.

Bulletin Board: Cover background with cranberry and tan wrapping paper. Pin a real straw hat with cranberry ribbon to the board. May want to garnish with tan dried baby's breath. Make lettering on the board the reverse of whatever is the main background color of the wrapping paper background (i.e., cranberry background—tan lettering; tan background—cranberry lettering).

Poster: Cut tan poster board in the shape of a hat. Garnish with print craft ribbon. Write information on the brim.

Registration

Table Decoration: Cover the table with a cranberry tablecloth. Construct a hat box with a cranberry and tan print (use wallpaper). Place various hats on a small hat tree. Make sure each person at the table is wearing a hat.

Sign-up Sheet/Poster:
1. Use tan parchment paper with calligraphied headers and bond with tiny cranberry ribbon.
2. Construct hat from tan card stock and a paper bowl. Garnish with flowers and ribbon. Have people sign on the brim.

Name Tags: Make tiny three-dimensional hats by painting egg holders (from paper egg cartons) white. Glue them to index card stock that has been trimmed into a round/oval shape. Glue on band and bow using various colored printed craft ribbon. Insert hat pin. Names are written on brims.

Refreshments

Menu: Cold marinated chicken on bed of greens
             Cranberry bread
             Fresh fruit
             Dessert:
                Fashion little cakes into hats. Use icing to make band and bow.

Drinks: Coffee
             Cranberry punch

Style of Service: Served by the plate. Hostess/waitresses should be wearing hats.

Decorations

Walls: Hang large straw hats decorated with ribbons and silk flowers.

Windows: Cranberry tapers with print craft ribbon bows and baby's breath.

Stage/Front: Set up puppet theater to look like a closet and center it on the stage. Situate tall hat trees on either side. Place a large cranberry floral bouquet in front of the podium.

Banquet Tables: Arrange separately.
- *Tablecloth:* Wheat colored paper tablecloths
- *Plates/Napkins:* Cranberry
- *Cups:* Clear tumblers or cranberry colored stock
- *Nut Cups:* Fashion hat boxes out of pieces of paper towel tubing covered with cranberry and wheat print wallpaper. Fill with nuts and mints.
- *Place Cards:* Tan card stock decorated with a tiny satin bow.

- *Programs:* Cut index card stock into circles (4 to 5 inches in diameter). Turn a nut cup upside down and glue to form the crown of a hat. Spray paint them tan. Glue on printed craft ribbon to form the band and bow. Staple or pin to plain circle backing and insides.
- *Centerpieces:* Place medium-sized straw hats with tiny satin ribbon and dried baby's breath on the center of the tables. Place a tall cranberry taper on either side of the hat.

Agenda

Schedule: 11:00 A.M.–1:00 P.M.

Time	Activity	Duration
11:00	Hat Contest	10 min.
11:10	Welcome/prayer	5 min.
11:15	Musical Hats	10 min.
11:25	Door prizes	10 min.
11:35	Hat fashion show	15 min.
11:50	Lunch	30 min.
12:20	Special music	5 min.
12:25	Puppet Show—Tale of Two Hats	15 min.
12:40	Devotional	15 min.
12:55	Song	5 min.
1:00	Close	

Music:
  Background Music: Light and cheerful instrumental
  Special Music:
  1. "In Heaven's Eyes" by Phill McHugh (published by River Oaks Music)
  2. "The Day He Wore My Crown" by Phil Johnson (published by Justin Time Music)
     (If using this song, make sure to use it at the very end as a closure. It is beautiful but sober, not a good lead-in to the hat puppet show.)
Activity Ideas:
  - *Hat contest:* Encourage guests to wear hats. During the presession time, give each guest a ballot to vote for the best hat in various categories, such as the prettiest, funniest, most original, etc. Collect secret ballots, tabulate, and present winners with prizes just before lunch.
  - *Musical Hats:* Have guests remove good hats and stand in a circle, each

121

facing the other's back. If the group is large, have a volunteer from each table. Provide battered hats for all contestants except one. When the music starts, each contestant will grab the hat from the woman in front of her and place it on her head. When the music stops, whoever is not wearing a hat is out. Continue until only one is left. Award prize.

- *Hat Fashion Show:* Put together a fashion show tracing the styles of hats through history. This can be done comically or seriously. End with a creation of the hat of the future.
- *Door Prizes:* Award prizes for questions about moms and daughters. As a tie breaker, award prize to the first one with her hand up. For example:
    1. Which mom got up the most times last night with a little one?
    2. Which mother and daughter have birthdays closest together on the calendar?

    Or you can fashion questions around hats. For example:
    1. A bride would wear a . . . (wedding veil).
    2. A little boy going to Little League would put on a . . . (baseball hat).
    3. Jackie Kennedy was famous for wearing a . . . (pillbox hat).
    4. The scarf women use to cover their hair when working is called a . . . (bandana).
    5. Type of hat that shades the eyes without covering the head is called a . . . (visor).
- *Puppet Show:* Tale of Two Hats

Need:	Two hats, one with a feather and one with a net. Use felt to make eyes and faces. Wire them into stick puppets. Also needed are a glove and a boot, soap flakes, and a bucket of water. Some sort of screen is also needed to shield puppeteers.

* * *

Narrator:	Once upon a time, not so long ago, there lived two beautiful hats in the northeast corner of a cozy little closet. The first was a lovely hat *(show feathered hat)* called Fluffy because she possessed the most gorgeous plume. She would look so chic whenever her mistress would take her for a walk. Her roommate, Netty *(show net hat),* had a delicate blue and green net that softly swayed in the breeze. One day they started to discuss the other inhabitants of the closet.
Netty:	Your feather is looking very jaunty today.
Fluffy:	Your net is so becoming. The mistress looks so elegant when she puts you on. I can't understand why she doesn't wear us more often. We make her look so snazzy!
Netty:	That old yarn hat, who lives on the second shelf, makes our mistress look like a mitten! You can't even see her ears and hardly even her eyes.
Fluffy:	Yarny is bad but that rain hat, Dribbles, is really drab—no color, not even a feather!
Netty:	Our mistress must wear them to be kind, their being so ugly and all.

122

Narrator: So those two hats decided, for the good of their mistress, that they would solve her problem. They enlisted Bert the Boot to escort these ugly hats away. *(Use boot to kick hats out . . . but do not kick too far because Miss Glove needs to be able to retrieve them. May want to use little screams.)* After all, their mistress had Netty and Fluffy, and these other hats were not necessary.

One cold morning the mistress, not seeing her yarn hat, grabbed Netty *(take Netty away and put soap flakes on her)* and went out. Several hours later Netty returned in tears and was shaking uncontrollably.

Netty: *(Shake so flakes fly. Use tearful voice.)* Please go ask Sylvia Scarf to come over. I'm freezing! It's cold out there and the wind blew my net to pieces! And on top of freezing my stitching, I have utterly failed our mistress.

Fluffy: No!

Netty: I couldn't reach her ears and she was so cold, we had to come home early.

Narrator: The next day the mistress grabbed Fluffy and went out to work. *(Take Fluffy away and submerge in bucket of water.)* And when they returned, Fluffy was a sight to behold. She was drenched, and her beautiful plume was bedraggled.

Netty: Oh, my dear Fluffy, what happened?

Fluffy: It is wet outside. Do you know that the sky drips! I'm ruined; I'm soaked to my lining!

Netty: Fluffy, my dear, I think we need to reconsider our position on those other hats. They aren't as pretty as us, but they sure can take care of some areas that we cannot.

Fluffy: Yes, I think I understand the mistress' purposes now. She wears us when she feels bouncy or dramatic, but those other hats keep her warm and dry. They aren't like us, but their jobs are none the less important.

Narrator: So Netty and Fluffy went to Gloria Glove and asked her to fetch the other hats. After apologies were given and accepted, peace again reigned in the cozy little closet.

People many times fall into the same trap as Netty and Fluffy. They see others with different gifts and talents and either get critical or depressed when they compare them to their own. The Lord created us to work interdependently to further His Kingdom. *(May want to read and discuss 1 Cor. 12.)* Let us rejoice in our differences and each seek to find out the task God has given us to do at this time. Then let us do it wholeheartedly (Col. 3:23).

Evangelistic Outreach Workshop/Banquet

Event: *Banquet or Workshop Dinner*
Theme: *Vegetable Gardening*
Title: *Outreach Workshop*
              Hoedown Dinner
Audience: *All church*
Goal: *Instruction, pep rally, fellowship*
Color: *Green and brown*
Mood: *Cute, earthy*
Motif: *Vegetables, watering cans, fertilizer, dirt, seeds, soil, trowels*
Message: *This is an excellent theme to use to focus attention on outreach. This event could be adapted to a workshop with various subjects pertaining to witnessing.*

This theme also works well communicating that the things people plant and cultivate in their minds are the things that are going to grow in their lives.

Publicity

Announcement Ideas:
1. Person could make the announcement in overalls and a straw hat.
2. Each week the pastor could lift out from behind the podium a different planting item, introducing the announcement.

Invitations: Make carrots of orange card stock. Punch a hole in the top and tie on green yarn for tops. Print information on carrot. Fold and staple brown construction paper into an envelope and bury the carrot, leaving top out.

Bulletin Board/Poster: Construct a garden scene out of construction paper. Use construction and tissue paper to create various vegetables. Write information on seeds and in the sky.

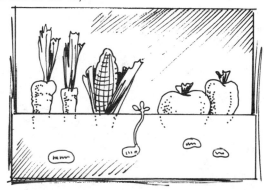

Registration

Registration Table Decorations: Set a basket of fresh vegetables on a green tablecloth.
Sign-up Sheet/Poster:
1. White paper with pictures of vegetables on border. (Check out the clip art books.)
2. Brown paper sack laid flat on table.
3. Cut out construction paper pumpkins with curly wire vines.

Name Tags: Create various vegetables out of card stock. Curl wire to make vine on pumpkin. Add yarn to carrots and radishes to make tops. Garnish little lettuce heads with green tissue. These can be presented in a creative way using a small portable bulletin board. Cut strips of paper (brown paper sacks work great) in a wavy pattern. Staple them on to the bulletin board so that they overlap and form long rows of pockets. Place the name tags in these pockets to give the illusion of plants growing in soil.

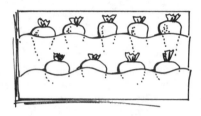

Refreshments

Menu: Potluck
Baked beans
Baked potatoes
Lots of salads

Drinks: Green punch
Iced tea
Coffee

Style of Service: Buffet. Servers manning the buffet table and punch bowl should be dressed in denim overalls and straw hats. Or they could be wearing matching tie-dyed shirts and bandanas.

Decorations

Outdoor Entrance: Hay bales, tools
Greeters: Dressed in overalls and straw hats, handing out programs
Walls: Large vegetables (perhaps cartooned) made from poster board
Windows: Large green candles garnished with vegetables
Displays: Wheelbarrow with vegetables or a shrub in it
Serving Table: Green tablecloth with watering can for a centerpiece
Front: Paint farm and barn scene. Stack bales of hay and make a scarecrow. In front of podium place a bouquet made from vegetables.
Banquet Tables:
• *Tablecloth:* Brown

- *Plates/Napkins:* Bright kelly green
- *Cups:* Use Mason jars without the lids.
- *Flatware:* Set out on table, perch napkin in the fork and set in a Mason jar.
- *Nut Cups:* Starter potting pots (peat or plastic) with green tissue and peanuts.
- *Centerpiece:* Put a clay pot in the center with a parsley plant in it. Stick humorous plant IDs in pot (*Lettuce* go and tell others, *Peas* go with us, *Bean* too busy to witness, or *Squash* down all fear). Add other items like garden gloves, trowels, seed envelopes, bags of seeds as you see fit.

- *Programs:* Print up on white envelopes, making them look like seed packets. Insert program (if dealing with evangelism, you might want to include tracts and invitations to church). Throw in a couple of seeds for effect!

Agenda

Schedule A: Outreach Workshop   8:30 A.M.–1:30 P.M.

Time	Activity	Duration
8:30	Donuts and coffee	30 min.
9:00	Session One	45 min.
10:00	Workshop A	45 min.
*11:00	Workshop B	45 min.
*12:00	Lunch	30 min.
12:30	Special music	10 min.
12:40	Session Two	50 min.
1:30	Close	

* Note 15 minute passing time between workshops and before lunch.

Music:

- *Background Music:* Country instrumentals (play softly or it will become too busy); tunes like "Turkey in the Straw" are good.
- *Special Music Suggestions:* "Who's Gonna Carry the Light?" by Squire Parson (published by Beulah Music).

Activity Ideas:

- *Session One:* Pastor or others may make good use of the gardening motif to explain how to share God's truth with someone. Cultivating friendships. Removing the rocks of misconceptions about God. Plants do not grow overnight. Patience is required. Frequent watering is necessary, etc.
- *Session Two:* Pastor may want to lay out his vision, plan, or strategy for outreach in the upcoming months.
- *Skit:*
  1. Dramatize the Parable of the Sower.
  2. Role play various witnessing situations.
- *Workshop Topic Ideas:*
  Dealing with Difficult Questions
  Witnessing in the Workplace
  Outreach in the Neighborhoods
  Hospital Sunshine Ministry
  Setting Up Ministry Groups
  Organizing a Home Children's Bible Club
  The How-To's of Prison Ministry
  Letter Evangelism
  (Use as a training session for outreach groups to present their programs.)

  For Children:
  How to Witness to My Friends
  Making and Using a Wordless Book
  Games/Peanut Hunt/Planting Real Seeds

Schedule B: Banquet   6:00–8:00 P.M.

Time	Activity	Duration
6:00	Pickle Contest/Bean Plant	15 min.
6:15	Welcome/prayer	5 min.
6:20	Peanut Hunt	15 min.
6:35	Dinner	40 min.
7:15	Thank-you's	5 min.
7:20	Puppet Show	30 min.
7:50	Devotional	10 min.
8:00	Close	

Activity Ideas:

- *Pickle Contest:* Have homemade or store-bought pickles. Have guests taste pickles and cast ballots for the best. Can also be widened to include other home-baked goods. (Have items numbered and use secret ballots to avoid any problems with hurt feelings.)

- *Bean Plant:* Set up manned table with cups, dirt, and bean seeds. Have children plant a bean when they first arrive.
- *Peanut Hunt:* Divide all children into five to ten groups. Assign a captain for each group. Give each group a barnyard animal name. Only the captain may touch the peanuts. Children hunt peanuts; when they find some, they must yell the animal sound loudly to attract the attention of their captain. He then comes and picks up the peanuts. Team with the most peanuts wins. This game works well outside or inside (but it is loud).
- *Puppet Show:* Use the script from *Ants'hillvania* (written by Jimmy and Carol Owens with Cherry Boone O'Neill, put out by Birdwing Records).
- *Devotional:* Coordinate with puppet show. Draw out applications.

Picnic

Event:	*Picnic*
Theme:	*Ants*
Title:	*All Church Labor Day Picnic*
Audience:	*All ages*
Goal:	*Instruction, evangelism, recreation, fellowship*
Color:	*Red, white, and black*
Mood:	*Cute, crisp, refreshing*
Motif:	*Ants, bug spray, knives, forks, picnic baskets*
Message:	*Like the ants, let's labor to serve the Lord while we have opportunity.*

Publicity

Announcement Ideas:
1. Place a picnic basket on the podium with a red checkered cloth. Place in it various items that will need to be brought to the picnic (swimsuit, money, play food to represent real food, etc.). Have pastor open the basket and talk about the picnic as he pulls things out of the basket.
2. Have someone dress like an ant and invite everyone to the picnic because he is *hungry!* Have him stress (tongue in cheek) that no bug spray is allowed! (Ant outfit: black sweatsuit, antennae made of pipe cleaners, and pom-pom balls.)
3. Compose an ant marching song to the tune of "When Johnny Comes Marching Home." Alter the words to include information about the picnic. Choreograph marching ants (people in black sweats and antennae). For example:

	The ants go marching one by one, hurrah, hurrah. *(Sing two times, one person could sing second hurrah as an echo.)*
	The ants go marching one by one,
(1)	September third to the picnic come!
	And we'll all have fun when the picnic is finally here!
(2)	Bring ma and pa and the little ones too.
(3)	It costs two bucks, did you think it was free?
(4)	There'll be food, swimming, games, and more.
(5)	Into the water you all can dive.
(6)	Roasting marshmallows on some sticks.
(7)	We'll talk about the Lord in heaven.
(8)	It starts at one, so don't be late.
(9)	There's lots of food on which to dine.
(10)	There'll be volleyball for the men.

Flyers/Invitations: Paste white paper on red construction paper forming a red border. Letter information on paper in black. You may wish to cut away a corner of the invitation to look as though an ant chomped off a piece.

Bulletin Board/Poster Ideas:
1. Cover background of board with red and white checkered paper/fabric. Attach three-dimensional ants (made from Legg's eggs and pipe cleaners) with plastic forks and knives in hands.

2. Have lines of construction paper ants on walls. On each back is a piece of food: cupcake, apple, pie, etc. (made from construction paper). On the food items, write information concerning the picnic.

Registration

Registration Table Decorations: Place a red and white gingham cloth on the table. Set a large picnic basket on the table with a red and white checked cloth napkin in it. Make an ant out of black Legg's eggs (stocking carton) and pipe cleaners (use large wiggle eyes). Have the ant hold a small poster board that contains information concerning the event. Cut a corner of the poster to look like the ant chomped off a piece.

Programs: Although programs usually fall under the auspices of the decorations committee, I have found them much more helpful at picnics if they are made into information packets to be given out (one per family) upon registration. Include a schedule, a list of items to bring, and perhaps a map with directions to the picnic grounds.

Sign-Up Sheet: Center white paper on red poster board to create a red border around the paper. Add a troop of marching ants on the bottom, if desired.

Name Tags: Name tags are not necessary at a picnic but, if desired, simple red and white stickers would work well.

Decorations

Tablecloth: Red and white checkered

Plates/Napkins: White. (Have extra on hand; remember that watermelon is being served later and some folks may want plates or at least napkins for that.)

Flatware: White plastic flatware could be set out on the serving table in small plastic bins.

Cups: Cups are not necessary if everyone brings soft drinks in cans. However, a pack of medium/small cups could be helpful for moms who want to split a can among their children.

Centerpieces:
1. White potted mums with red bows (later plant at church)
2. White/red flowers in mason jar (gathered from someone's garden)

Refreshments

Menu: Hamburgers
            Hot dogs
            Buns
            Potato chips
            Baked beans
            Assorted salads
            Cookies
            Brownies/bars
            Cupcakes
            Watermelon
            Marshmallows

Drinks: Soda/Juice

Condiments Needed: Pepper, salt, catsup, mustard, mayonnaise

Style of Service: Buffet

Form four serving lines with an even number of items on each table. Set up dessert table to the side so that people can come and go to that table when done with the meal. This will keep the lines moving.

Method of Acquiring Food: Assigned potluck

Equipment Needed:
Grills
Matches/lighter fluid
Sticks for marshmallows
Foil
Big baskets for buns (or serve meat in buns on platters)
Cookie sheets (to put meat on)
Sharp knives/serving spoons
Masking tape/pen (for labeling people's dishes and serving spoons)
Charcoal
Turners/pot holders
Paper towels

FROM START-UP TO CLEAN-UP

Agenda

Schedule: 1:00–6:30 P.M.

Time	Activity	Duration

1:00	Presession:
	    Bean Guess
	    Bubble Gum Blowing Contest
		30 min.

1:30	Eat	30+ min.
2:00	Games/Races:	30–60 min.

3:00	Free time:
	    Horseshoes
	    Volleyball
	    Softball
	    Swimming
	    Boat Rides
		2 hr.

5:00	Marshmallow roast/watermelon	30 min.

5:30	Campfire:
	    General sing
	    Thank-you/prizes
	    Skit
	    Special music
	    Devotional
		45 min.
		10 min.
		5 min.
		10 min.
		5 min.
		15 min.

6:15	Cleanup	15 min.
6:30	Head home	

Presession Activities:

These activities are designed to give people interesting things to do right away, as they arrive. Keep these activities close to the eating facilities so that your group congregates there. This is most helpful when trying to begin. It is very hard to gather people at a picnic when they have scattered to the four winds.

- *Bean Guess:* Fill a mason jar with beans or popcorn and have people write guesses as to how many are in the jar. The entry that comes the closest wins. (Make sure to really count the beans; don't estimate. Believe me, they will call you on it!)
- *Bubble Gum Blowing Contest.* Give each contestant a piece of gum and give them three tries to blow a bubble. Record the best of their efforts. The person with the biggest bubble receives a prize awarded at the campfire.
- *Autograph Buffs:* Give paper and pencil to guests as they arrive. Tell them to collect as many autographs as they can. Just before dinner collect sheets. Tabulate scores and award prizes at campfire. This activity serves to break the ice and helps to prevent newcomers from feeling isolated.
- *Marshmallow Stuff:* The object of this contest is to see who can stuff the most marshmallows in his mouth at one time. Make sure to have enough marshmallows on hand. Record attempts and give prize at the campfire.

Games:

- *Number Elimination*   *Need:* Whistle

  Have everyone stand in the playing field (in no particular order). Yell out a number, such as, "Get in groups of three." Give five seconds for players to group themselves in correct amounts (groups must be touching). Any person not in a group or any group with the wrong number of people in it is eliminated and has to leave the playing field. Yell out another number, and repeat the process. The last two or three people to survive are winners.

- *Three-legged Race*   *Need:* Long rags in strips, one per couple (use rags, not string, or you will have bleeding ankles)

  Tie center legs together and have couples race across field. First pair to finish with their tie intact wins.

- *Musical Division*   *Need:* Slips of paper with titles of songs in a grab bag

  Use this game as a way to divide your group into four to six teams. Choose the same number of common songs as you want teams. Make sure teams are even. Write the title of the songs on slips of paper (one per player) and place in the grab bag. Players draw a title from the bag and start to hum that song. The object of the game is to gather all the people who are humming the same tune. The first team to gather all their members wins.

- *Wheelbarrow Race*   *Need:* Whistle

  Players are paired off. When the whistle blows, one player picks up the legs of the other, who runs on his hands across the field. First pair to finish wins.

- *Sack Race*   *Need:* Two sacks per team
  Whistle

  Teams line up on the starting line. The first two hoppers of each team are in sacks. When the whistle blows, the first player hops down the field, around a marker (chair, person, whatever), and back, then tags the second runner. The second runner starts hopping the course while the first player gives his sack to the third player. This continues until the last player has completed the course. The team that finishes first wins.

- *Inside Out Race*   *Need:* Whistle

  Teams line up one behind the other with legs straddled. The last person in line crawls under the row of leg bridges to the end, gets up quickly and straddles his legs to form a bridge. Second to last person in line may begin as soon as first person has gone under him. First line to have everyone crawl through wins.

- *Tug-of-War*   *Need:* Rope

  Mark a line in the center of the field. Place rope across the line. Have each team try to drag the other team across the line. To win, the last member of the opposing team needs to be pulled across the line.

Note: Suggested prize for races is a grab bag of individually wrapped candy (caramels, sweet tarts, tootsie rolls, etc.). Let each winning player reach in and grab one. Award candy at the end of each game or keep a running tally and award prize after games are completed.

You also will need a small bag of lime to mark the start and finish lines.

Skit:	**Anterprizing — To Be or Not to Be**
Characters:	Narrator
	Indy Ant
	Slug Ant
	Lady Indy
	Lady Slug
	Junior Indy
	Junior Slug
	(Ants can dress in black sweatsuits with antennae constructed of pipe cleaner and pom-pom balls. Neckties, aprons, and shorts with suspenders can be worn to differentiate between the characters.
Props:	Ant Hill—Construct from large cardboard carton
	Pillows in cases to represent sacks of food
	Paper snowflakes dangling on string from a pole
	Folding chairs, throw rugs, dust cloth
	Optional: TVs (use box with hanger antenna), and jug labeled "Bug Juice"
Narrator:	Once upon a time, on a grassy slope not so far away from your house, there lived two ants. The first was named Industri'Ant or Indy for short. The second was named Sluggard or Slug for short. (*Ants come out and wave.*)
	These ants had many things in common. They both lived in little hills of sand (*ants point to sand hills*) where they lived with their wives (*lady ants come out and curtsy or wave*) and their children (*junior ants come out and wave, blow bubbles, whatever . . . just do it simultaneously*). Each had three chairs, a rug, and a TV. Ants are fond of anything with antennae, you know. (*Have ants set up TV, rug, and three folding chairs.*)
	There was, however, one major difference. One family was very industrious (*they bow and busy themselves straightening the house*) while the other was . . . well . . . really quite . . . lazy (*lazy ants put hands on hips and look indignantly at narrator*). Well, you are.
Indy:	I hear that (*name of your group*) is holding a picnic at (*name of location*). Why don't you come with me on a scavenging mission. You know what great cooks those ladies over there are!
Slug:	Well, I don't know, Indy, it seems like a long way to go.
Indy:	You could work under the tables while I follow the one-year-olds around. They drop the best crumbs. If you get lucky and catch them asleep you can collect a feast from the stickiness on their hands alone!
Slug:	Sounds pretty dangerous to me. What if they lose their balance and sit on you?

136

Indy:	Usually their diapers have enough padding to allow escape. But you do have to watch out for running feet.
Slug:	Sorry, this doesn't sound like my cup of tea. But if you go, could you bring me back a bite of cake?
	(Exit daddy ants, enter lady ants with kids)
Lady Indy:	Would you like to run over to Mrs. Smith's *(or use name of someone at group)* kitchen with me this morning? I know of a quick little path that goes right to her pantry. And I am quite certain that the lid on her honey jar is not screwed on too tight. She is training her children to cook, you see.
Lady Slug:	No thanks, dear, you go on without me. My favorite soap opera, "As the Worm Turns," will be on shortly and I don't want to miss it. And I know you won't be back by the time "All My Aphids" comes on. Besides, I've heard tell that she's been known to use You-Know-What.
Lady Indy:	What?
Lady Slug:	*(Covers ears of her child and gives a knowing look)* R-A-I-D.
Lady Indy:	I'll be careful, but I think that is only a problem when everyone goes at once.
Lady Slug:	Well, suit yourself, it's your thorax . . . but if you go, would you mind bringing me back a smidgen of honey?
	(Lady ants exit, leaving kid ants)
Junior Indy:	I need to go over to Farmer Joe's garden and pick up some grain for my mom. Would you like to come along?
Junior Slug:	That stuff is for grown-ups to do. We can't possibly carry the loads that our fathers can carry. It's really not worth the bother. But if you do go, can you grab a piece of corn for me?
	(Exit ants)
Narrator:	*(As narrator talks, have the Industrious ants work steadily storing food by piling up pillows that can be scattered throughout the audience. The lazy family gathers sporadically, resting, playing, and drinking "Bug Juice.")*

As the summer waxed and waned, the Lazy ants rested and played while the Industrious ants worked ever so hard. At last winter came and snowed them all in. *(Attach snowflakes to string on a stick and dangle over the hills.)* Over at Indy's house they were snug little bugs in their rugs, happily watching reruns of "Victory Garden." The Lazy ant household was much different. They were cold and hungry and soon breathed their last. *(Lazy ants do dramatic death scenes and collapse in a pile.)*

The Bible speaks of such folly in Proverbs 6:6-8: "Go to the ant, thou sluggard; consider her ways and be wise, which having no guide, overseer, or ruler, provideth her food in the summer and gathereth her food in harvest. How long wilt thou sleep, O sluggard? When wilt thou arise out of thy sleep?"

And in John 9:4: "We must work the works of Him that sent Me, while it is day; the night cometh, when no man can work."

Which ant family are you like?

Adult Social

Event:	*Adult Social*
Theme:	*Escape*
Title:	*The Late Great Adult Escape!*
Audience:	*Adults*
Goal:	*Recreation, fellowship, encouragement*
Color:	*Optional (match up with paper goods)*
Mood:	*Light, fun*
Motif:	*Jailbreak, guards, handcuffs, locks*
Message:	*The Lord provides an escape or strength for us when situations become overbearing.*

Publicity

Announcement Ideas:

1. Have children and teens dressed as police looking for "them." After scouring the auditorium shouting such words as "Have you seen them?" or "No sign of them yet!" have one official-looking teen put out an all points bulletin for parents. Can sound something like this: "Calling all cars. Calling all cars. We are reporting parents missing. Last seen tucking unsuspecting children in bed. Allegedly leaving cheerleading dress unmade, homework unchecked, and house in disaster. A parent can be identified by the wild gleam in eyes of an otherwise frazzled grown-up. Rumor has it that they will be congregating on *(event date)* with large numbers of other wired adults acting in ways that are usually reserved for us, the youth of the country. This must not be allowed to happen. If given too much of a taste of freedom, they will give up car pool duty forever. Report all sightings to "The Committee to Stop Adult Silliness."

Flyers/Invitations: Have information written on little slips of paper. Have someone at door (wearing sunglasses and a trench coat) furtively passing out the invitations with the attitude of, "Shhhh . . . don't tell the kids."

Bulletin Board/Poster Ideas:

1. Create prison break scene on bulletin board with real wire to give it texture.
2. Cut a poster in jagged halves. Write information on either side. Cut the word "escape" out of red construction paper and place on the wall between the two pieces.

3. Hang a 2' by 3' piece of wire fencing on the wall. Write information on white/black/red paper and attach to the wire.

Registration

Registration Table Decorations: Use a black and white geometric print tablecloth.

1. (Unconventional approach) Make a model of a prison or fort (made from cardboard box). Attach long thin wire springs to it, with little paper cutouts in the shape of running adults taped to ends.

2. (More sophisticated approach) Place black vase with red flowers on table.

Sign-up Sheet: Have people sign up on little slips of paper and slip them in a tin cup or other container.

Name Tags: Use white stickers to make prisoner I.D. numbers. Use thick black marker to write the first three letters of last name plus phone number. Place first name underneath.

Refreshments

Menu: Chips and dip
Veggie platter
Cheese and crackers
Brownies and bars
Fondue pot
Stuffed mushrooms
Little sandwiches
Cookies

Drinks: Decaf coffee
Soft drinks

Condiments Needed: Sugar, cream, ice
Style of Service: Buffet

Decorations

Buffet Table:
- *Plates/Napkins/Cups:* Black
- *Tablecloth:* White or black and white geometric print
- *Centerpiece:* Large floral bouquet of bright scarlet red. Put in a black or black and white vase (stripes, checks, or other geometric design would look great).

Room Arrangement: Buffet table in front with podium. Tables grouped around edges of room, allowing room for games in center.

Agenda

Schedule: 7:30–9:30 P.M.

Time	Activity	Duration
7:30	Presession activity	15 min.
7:45	Welcome	5 min.
7:50	Games	40 min.
8:30	Refreshments	30 min.
9:00	Sing and Share	10 min.
9:10	Special Music	5 min.
9:15	Devotional	15 min.
9:30	Prayer/Close	

Presession Activities:
- *Who Am I?* As people enter the room, pin the name of a Bible character on their backs. Have people ask questions needing only yes and no answers to try to figure out who they are. Possible characters:

Isaac	Ishmael	Samson	Delilah	Ananias
Sapphira	Eunice	David	Silas	Paul
Eli	Mary	Martha	Naaman	Jacob
Esau	Abraham	Moses	Peter	John
Adam	Eve	Goliath	Priscilla	Joseph
Naomi	Ruth	Andrew	Cain	Abel
Joshua	Caleb	Solomon	Elizabeth	Esther
Elijah	Lot	Aaron	Aquila	Nebuchadnezzar
Mordecai	Nehemiah	Ezra	Jonah	Sarah
Daniel	Bathsheba	Saul	Pilate	Miriam

- *Incognito:* Enlist the aid of three early guests to circulate among arriving guests and give them fictitious identities. One is to give each guest a name. The second tells each guest where he was born and the last tells people what their favorite hobby is. When most of the guests arrive have everyone stand in a circle and introduce themselves by their new identities. Could introduce this activity by mentioning that every es-

141

caping convict needs a new identity. For example: I'm Mickey Mouse, I was born in Toledo, and I like to knit.

- *Games and Activity Descriptions:* You will not have time in the period allotted to do all these games. Pick those games suitable to the character of your group. Save the wilder and messier games for the end.
- *Verse Match:* Pass out verse fragments to group (four different verses or groups of verses). Have people group themselves in order to put the verse together. First team to complete its verse wins.
- *Mummy Wrap Race:* Give each team a roll or two of bathroom paper. When whistle blows, each team wraps one of its members so that no part of that person's body shows. First team done wins.
- *Verse Clue Treasure Hunt:* Use Bible verses to give clues as to where to find a treasure. Each team follows a different path to the same prize. Whichever team gets there first gets the prize. For example, a clue might be Genesis 37:3 (Joseph's coat of many colors). Hang a brightly colored coat (add stripes with colored vinyl tape) in coat closet with the next verse clue in a pocket.
- *Hot Hands:* Give each team an ice cube of equal size. Team must melt ice cube using only their hands. First team to liquefy ice cube wins.
- *Personal Scavenger Hunt:* Yell out various groups of objects that people have on hand (comb in a shoe). The first team to bring the required item to emcee gets a point. Winner is team with most points. Emcee must stand at an equal distance from all teams.

Personal Scavenger Hunt List:
1. Three shoelaces tied together
2. Three lipstick tubes in a cup
3. Used gum in paper
4. Paper clip, safety pin, and bobby pin attached together
5. Three rings in a shoe
6. Two quarters and a store receipt
7. A shirt buttoned up and turned inside out
8. Three different socks stuffed inside each other
9. Antacid or aspirin wrapped in a tissue
10. A belt looped through the arm of a jacket and buckled
11. Five dollar bill tucked inside a Bible
12. A comb tucked inside a checkbook
13. A used hankie or tissue
14. Nail file in an envelope
15. Scissors and five pennies
16. Keys in a hat

- *Surprise Observation:* At some point during the evening, perhaps while explaining rules for a game, have a group of weirdly dressed people rush through the room. Have them wear strange socks, wigs, outlandish hats, and chase each other with a rubber snake. They must be unannounced and totally unexpected for best results. After they have run around for a while and left, pass out paper and pencil and ask guests to answer various questions concerning what they saw. (*What type of footwear was the girl wearing?*) Score and award prize to the winner.

The next games are messy. Depending on the character of your group, you may choose to substitute them with other games. Make sure to use a tarp. Have towels on hand for cleanup. Garbage bags can be used with a hole cut in top for protection of clothes.

- *Coke Joke:* A guy from each team lays down and puts an empty Coke bottle on his head. A girl from each team tries to fill the bottle by pouring water into it from a bucket.
- *Russian Roulette for the Chicken Hearted:* Draft four guys, one from each team. Have them choose an egg (one raw, three hard-boiled). Draft four women volunteers. Upon signal, women smash the eggs over the heads of the men. Give extra points to the team that chose the raw egg.
- *Barber Shop:* Draft volunteers from each team, one guy and one girl. Cover the guys with tarp and sit them down in "barber shop chairs." Have men hold an inflated balloon in their mouths. Squirt an even portion of shaving cream on each balloon. Blindfold the girls and have them try to scrape off shaving cream with a straightedge razor. Best job or survivor wins.

Wedding Shower

Event: *Wedding Shower*
Theme: *Wedding*
Title: *(Name) Wedding Shower Brunch*
Audience: *Invite all ladies of the church*
Goal: *Celebration*
Color: *Colors of the wedding*
Mood: *Pretty, fancy, hopeful*
Motif: *Wedding gown, veil, white lace, rings, flowers, new home, wedding cake, doves, hearts*
Message: *Proverbs 14:1: Wise women build their homes, foolish women tear their homes down with their own hands. Discuss the building blocks for a sturdy marriage (patience, understanding, etc.).*

Publicity/Registration

Usually showers are done as surprises so most of the publicity will be via word of mouth, invitation, and phone. Registration is done on the phone via RSVP.

Invitations:

1. Wedding bells can be made by cutting white doilies into a bell shape and attaching information sheets to them with a tiny satin bow.

2. Wedding cake invitations can be fashioned by cutting white card stock into three tiers. Garnish with tiny flat lace. Staple onto information pages.

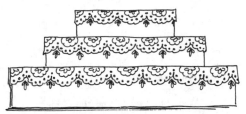

3. Write/paste information in the center of a lacy heart.

Name Tags: If name tags are desired, write names in fancy script on white card stock. Attach to a pick and stick in a tiny corsage (see Agenda).

Decorations

Windows/Ceiling: Drape crepe paper or ribbon. Hang bunches of white balloons. Use colors of the wedding.

Stage/Front: Decorate a chair with bows and ribbon. Do not put the bride too far from other people or she will feel isolated and uncomfortable.
Buffet Tablecloth: Use the colors of the wedding. A lace overlay is usually very pretty.
Plates/Napkins: Use the colors of the wedding or buy wedding print paper goods.
Flatware: Wrapped in napkin and tied with a tiny satin ribbon
Cups: Clear tumblers or assorted china
Centerpiece:
1. Flower arrangement in a china teacup.
2. Bride doll
3. Bridal headpiece and veil on table hat stand with flower petals.
4. Wedding cake made of white towels rolled around each other, decorated with silk flowers and ribbon.

Refreshments

Menu: Decorated cake
Coffee cake
Tea breads
Rolls/danish
Omelet (see Agenda–Egg Relay)
Fruit tray
Mini quiche

Drinks Coffee
Tea
Punch (color coordinate if possible)
Style of Service: Buffet
Method of Acquiring Food: Committee catered
Condiments Needed: Cream, butter, sugar
Equipment Needed: Cutting knife, cake server, coffee maker, teapot, punch bowl, ladle. Use crystal with silver serving platters.

Agenda

Schedule: 9:30–11:30 A.M.

Time	Activity	Duration
9:30	Mixer (see below)	15 min.
9:45	Welcome/prayer	5 min.
9:50	How Well Do You Know the Bride?	10 min.
10:00	Egg Relay	10 min.
10:10	Dress the Bride	15 min.
10:25	Eat	20 min.
10:45	Devotional	15 min.
11:00	Open presents	30 min.
11:30	Pray/close	

Activities and Game Descriptions:

Corsages: As guests arrive, give each person a little corsage as a favor. Make them from real or silk flowers. Make the bride's corsage white. Use different color ribbon that can be later used to separate group into teams (four colors of ribbon if four teams are needed, five colors if five teams are needed).

Mixer: (Choose one)

1. *What Is It?* Lay out on a table various ingredients and substances (nothing poisonous). Put each substance in a paper cup and place on a separate numbered piece of construction paper. As guests come in give them a numbered sheet of paper and a pencil and have them try to identify the substance by smelling, shaking, tasting, or whatever.

   Substance Ideas: Sugar, salt, soda, baking powder, cream of tartar, cloves, allspice, ginger, basil, parsley, dill weed, talcum powder, laundry detergent, soft soap, lotion, toothpaste, suntan lotion, etc.

2. *Slogans:* Paste product slogans to construction paper, one per paper. Number and lay out on a table. As people come in, give them a numbered piece of paper and have them try to identify the products and match the slogans.

Welcome and Prayer: It is a nice touch (if parties are able and willing) to have the mother of the bride prepare the opening prayer and the groom's mom, the closing prayer.

After welcoming the guests the emcee can give the correct answers on the mixer game. She can then split the group into teams by color of ribbon on corsage. If desired, a running team score can be started by totaling points on the mixer game. Tally score after each game. The team with the most points goes to the refreshment table first.

Team games:

- *Egg Relay:* Provide eggs (one per participant) and bowl for each team. Guests run up and crack egg one-handed into bowl. Then they dash back to tag the next player. When all the lines are finished total up score as follows:

  Team finishing first–10 points

  Team finishing second–5 points

  Give each team 2 points for each unbroken egg yoke in bowl.

  Lose 5 points if there is any broken shell in bowl.

  Total up score. Team with the most points wins. If eggs are usable, make into an omelet and serve at brunch.

- *Dress the Bride:* Give each team white tissue paper, crepe paper (sheets), tape, and scissors. Assign each team part of a wedding gown; skirt, bodice, sleeves, headpiece, veil, and wedding bouquet. Give them fifteen minutes to create their section and then put the dress together on the bride and take a picture. If larger crowd, buy colored tissue and crepe paper and have them design maid of honor's dress as well.

- *How Well Do You Know the Bride?* Prepare a list of questions, either true or false, or which use simple word answers. These questions concern the bride's likes and dislikes and her past. Include some embarrassing moments wrestled from her mom. Be careful that the questions are not too embarrassing for the bride; we really do not want to spoil her day. To correct, ask the bride for the right answers. Total team score or award prize individually.

Examples:
1. The bride's favorite color is _____.
2. The bride's favorite subject in school was _____.
3. The bride kissed a snake for a nickel when she was five. (T/F)
4. How old was the bride when she had her first kiss?
5. What would be the bride's choice of vacation spots: Hawaii, Europe, Florida, Far East?
6. What is the bride's favorite household chore: dishes, laundry, grocery shopping?
7. Where did the bride meet the groom? School hall, church social, ocean, pool.
8. Favorite object when the bride was a child was: pillow, blanket, or stuffed animal?
9. Favorite story as a child: Winnie the Pooh, By Wagon Trails to Oregon, or (her favorite found out from mom)?
10. Bride accepted the Lord as her Saviour at age fourteen. (T/F)

Alternate Games:
- *1. Cake Make:* Have the bride frost and decorate a cake blindfolded.
- *2. Ring on a String:* Place a ring on a string and tie ends together forming large loop. Have all guests hold the string with hands forming fists. Have everyone move hands back and forth passing the ring around the circle (keep it moving). Place bride in middle of circle. She tries to guess where the ring is. Deduct points from team of guest caught with ring. Give points to team if they were guessed falsely. If bride hasn't guessed correctly in three guesses, the team holding the ring at time of third guess gets five points. Repeat with maid-of-honor in center. For larger crowds put more than one ring on the string.
- *3. Dream House Hunt:* Give each team a stack of magazines or catalogs, glue, scissors, and poster board with the outline of a house with designated blank rooms. Have each team hunt for needed rooms in magazines. The team that first completes the poster, with pictures of rooms glued in the correct spots, wins.
- *4. Bride's First Cake Recipe:* Place guests in circle. Give each guest a slip of paper which is one of two colors. Make sure to alternate colors. Everyone with "pink" piece of paper will write down an amount (e.g., 1 tsp. or 4 cups or 3 lbs.). Those with the "green" slips of paper write down an ingredient (flour, sugar, molasses, etc.). Then compose a "Mother-in-law's Secret Recipe" by having the first guest read her amount and the second guest read the ingredient. (1 cup salt, 2 tsp. chili powder, etc.). The third guest reads her amount, the fourth guest reads her ingredient, and so forth.
- *5. Word Creation:* Give to each guest a paper with the bride's name written out, including maiden name and new last name. Give guests five minutes to come up with as many words as they can think of using only those letters in name.

A Baby Shower

Event:	*Baby Shower*
Theme:	*Baby*
Title:	*Blessings in Pink and Blue*
Audience:	*All the women of the church who care to come.*
Goal:	*Celebration, encouragement*
Color:	*Pink and blue or colors of the nursery*
Mood:	*Soft, cuddly, gentle*
Motif:	*Bunnies, teddy bears, blocks, bottle, pacifier, diapers, pins, sleepers, stuffed animals, high chairs, playpen, stroller, crib, cradle (use motif found on plates)*
Message:	*Godly advice to new mom*

Publicity/Registration

Check by phone as to who is planning to come or write RSVP on invitations.

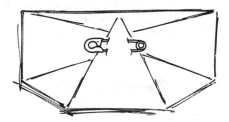

Invitations:

1. Diapers: Create invitations to look like diapers. Use a triangle of white paper and fold to form the diaper. Fasten with a small gold safety pin. Have information printed on the inside.
2. Baby Gown: Make baby gown invitations by cutting two doilies to form a gown. Make a tiny slit at the neckline and fold back to form a collar. Garnish with a tiny blue or pink bow. White paper is cut to look like a slip. Print information on this folded paper atttached underneath.

Name Tags:

1. Tiny diapers can be made out of white construction paper attached with tiny gold pins.
2. Baby bonnets can be formed from white card stock and bits of doily, lace, and ribbon.
3. Bibs can be created out of construction paper. Trim with doilies.

Decorations

Ceiling: Crepe paper/ribbon and balloons.

Stage/Front: Next to the seat of honor, attach to the ceiling a large bouquet of balloons and ribbon with streamers reaching the table where presents are to be set. Attach several small presents to the ribbons, forming a shower over the display of gifts.

Buffet Table:
- *Tablecloth:* Blue with white lace overlay.
- *Napkins/Plates:* Pink
- *Flatware/Cups:* Place white plastic flatware in clear plastic tumblers with napkins.
- *Nut Cups:* Make triangular diapers out of six-inch squares of pink/white/blue flannel. Attach with a pin. Dip in paraffin wax and open them so that they stand. Cool and fill with nuts and pink/white mints.

Centerpieces:
1. Make three large baby blocks out of square cardboard boxes. Cut letters, numbers, and borders out of thin cork and paste on the boxes to give them a carved look. Color coordinate with paint.
2. Porcelain baby doll
3. Antique toys of any kind
4. Fluffy stuffed animals
5. Teddy bear with color-coordinated bow, holding helium balloons
6. Repeat the motif on the plates.

Refreshments

Menu: Decorated cake
           Tea sandwiches
           Relish tray
           Fruit tray
           Tea cookies
           Mini cheesecakes

Drinks: Coffee
           Tea
           Punch (pink)

Style of Service: Buffet

Method of Acquiring Food: Committee catered

Condiments Needed: Cream, butter, sugar

Agenda

Schedule: *7:30–9:00* P.M.

Time	Activity	Duration
7:30	Presession Activity	15 min.
	It's in the Bag	
7:45	Welcome/prayer	5 min.
7:50	Games	20 min.
8:10	Eat	15 min.
8:25	Devotional	10 min.
8:35	Open gifts	25 min.
9:00	Prayer/close	

Presession Activities:

- *Mother-to-Be's Corsage:* A cute corsage for the mother-to-be can be made from lacy baby socks, baby's breath, netting, and ribbon.
- *Father's Survival Pajamas:* Pin all kinds of baby equipment to a large night shirt and wrap it up to be opened during the gift-opening time.

Games:

- *It's in the Bag:* This game can be played two ways. If done during the presession, put ten to fifteen baby items in a large pillowcase (thermometer in a case, pacifier, bottle, diaper, toy, baby food jar, spoon, vitamin jar, changing mat, rattle, teething ring, brush and comb, booties, socks, toenail clipper, etc.). As guests arrive, give them a paper and pencil, and by feeling the outside of the pillowcase have them attempt to determine the contents. The person with the most correct guesses wins.

   If done as a race during game time, provide one pillowcase filled with the same items for each team. Give each team three to five minutes to figure out the contents of the bag without opening it. At end of time, team with most correct items wins.
- *Baby Name Contest:* Give each guest a pink and blue paper. List the letters of the alphabet vertically on each sheet. Give players five minutes to write down a name beginning with each letter of the alphabet. (Have them write down the first name that pops into their heads.) Write girls' names on pink sheet and boys' names on blue sheet. After five minutes, see how many match with the mother-to-be's list. Award prize.
- *Scrambled Words:* List scrambled baby words on paper and give five to ten minutes for guests to unscramble them. Correct and give prize to the one with the most right answers.
- *Midnight Tears:* Give guests a paper and pencil and instruct them to draw a picture of a baby in a crib crying. Then turn off the lights so that it is completely dark while they are trying to accomplish this task. Display the artwork and have guests vote on the best one (secret ballot) during refreshments. (Make sure to have guests write their names on back of paper.)
- *Diaper Relay:* Form teams of four to eight players. Have them sit next to each other in a straight line of chairs. Give the first person in each

151

line a large baby doll with cloth diapers. Upon signal she undiapers baby and gives it to the next player, who diapers baby and gives it to the next player, who undiapers baby, and so on. The first line to have everyone complete the task wins.

- *Nursery Rhyme Puzzle Race:* Have guests sit on the floor or at a table. Give each player an envelope with a nursery rhyme puzzle in it. These puzzles can be made from an inexpensive Mother Goose book. Paste pages to construction paper. Cut each picture in pieces (make sure to make the same amount of pieces for each puzzle). Upon signal, the players open envelopes and piece together puzzles. The first one to finish wins a prize.
- *Baby Memory:* Place baby items on a tray. Give people one minute to study the items. Cover tray and have guests write down as many items as they can remember. Award prize to the one with the longest correct list.
- *Baby Bottle Contest:* Ask for four volunteers. Tell the mother-to-be that we are now going to demonstrate bottle feeding techniques. Fill two small (4 oz.) bottles with Coke or other carbonated beverage. Put on juice-size nipples. Blindfold two of the volunteers and have them feed the other two (who must sit on their hands). Award prize to the team that finishes first.
- *Baby Who?* Place baby photos that guests have brought on numbered construction paper on a table (one to a sheet). Give paper to guests and see if they can identify the babies. Give prize to guest with most correct guesses.
- *Bible Baby Quiz:* Quiz guests on their knowledge of babies of the Bible. Award small prize to person who answers question correctly first.
  1. Boy king (Josiah)
  2. Baby in a basket (Moses)
  3. Answer to mother's prayer (Samuel)
  4. Firstborn (Cain)
  5. Hated by siblings (Joseph)
  6. Abraham's firstborn (Ishmael)
  7. First recorded twins (Esau and Jacob)
  8. Slew a giant (David)
  9. Crippled son of Jonathan (Mephibosheth)
  10. Raised from the dead (Jairus' daughter)
  11. Learned Scripture from mom and granny (Timothy)
  12. Nursery was a stable (Jesus)

Other Reading:

Goddard, Gloria and Clement Wood. *Let's Have a Good Time Tonight*. New York: Grosset and Dunlop, 1938.

Hohenstein, Mary. *A Compact Encyclopedia of Games, Games, Games*. Minneapolis: Bethany House Publishers, 1988.

Rice, Wayne and Mike Yaconelli. *Play It*. Grand Rapids, Michigan: Zondervan, 1986.